CORKED

Tales of Advantage in Competitive Sports

BRIAN J. LOVE
MICHAEL L. BURNS

FIFTH
AVENUE
PRESS

Corked: Tales of Advantage in Competitive Sports

Copyright© 2019 by Brian Love and Michael Burns

Fifth Avenue Press is a locally focused and publicly owned publishing imprint of the Ann Arbor District Library. It is dedicated to supporting the local writing community by promoting the production of original fiction, non-fiction and poetry written for children, teens and adults.

Printed in the United States of America

First Printing, 2019

ISBN: 978-1-947989-37-5 (Paperback); 978-1-947989-36-8 (Hardcover); 978-1-947989-38-2 (e-book)

Fifth Avenue Press

343 S Fifth Ave

Ann Arbor, MI 48104

fifthavenue.press

Editor

Ann Arbor District Library

Layout & Design

Ann Arbor District Library

To the fans, the players, and the team owners, probably in that order.

CONTENTS

PREFACE

When Brian wrote a single author textbook published two years ago, it was a long, painstaking, and lonely effort. The requirement for everything to be integrated at one time was a huge undertaking. Writing this book was a lot more fun! Brian and Michael are both long-time sports fanatics. They set out to look at competitive advantage from an entertaining and historical perspective.

The authors started collecting stories, and that is when this book began to take form. They found stories in every sport imaginable, from football to jai alai. They hope is that readers find these short stories insightful, entertaining, and thought provoking.

The authors are academics, analysts, and, more than anything, sports enthusiasts. They have long had an interest in competitive athletics and the fine line that often separates winning and losing. As much as sports have provided entertainment for the authors they have also given them a solid foundation in academics. Brian learned early multiplication scratching out his bowling score long before electronic scoring at a place called Blasers Bowling Alley. It had only 10 lanes and a small vending machine with candy. Growing up near Chicago, Brian learned division by calculating the earned run average of various struggling Cubs pitchers. Mike grew up a Detroit sports fanatic. He would dive into box scores in the morning newspapers to find deeper meaning of the previous night's games. Plus-minus and efficiency ratings were Mike's favorite early analytics. He has been watching the Red Wings for as long as he can remember. It was all good training for a careers in science and engineering.

In this book there is a focus on performance advantage in each chapter. The chapters are designed to be short, self-contained, and in no particular order. The theme of competitive advantage holds diverse sports together throughout the book, sports such as baseball, speedskating, curling, and cricket. Not everything has to do with home field advantage explicitly, but this topic is approached in several chapters in the book. There are a few short and entertaining stories to highlight each chapter.

This book touches on agronomy, physics, materials science, bioengineering, and data science to show there may be deeper linkages between how teams are assembled for particular sites and venues, how to maintain players more effectively for a particular team, and how armed with data of field and equipment conditions. Teams and individuals could achieve more wins and better performances.

Even through the content from this book is static, we want to engage with readers. At the website corkedthebook.com, readers can readily interact with the authors and find additional context. There is a growing FAQ list on the website, periodic blog comments, and more detailed author information. Please contact the authors with stories you'd like us to consider for inclusion should a second *Corked* book take shape. In discussing the book with others, the authors would get new stories in a similar vein that they had never heard about before. They would also welcome testimonials on how the book impacted you and your family. These sorts of books linking history with sport are natural entrees for multi-generational discussions between grandparents, kids, and grandkids. It would be great to hear about how new connections were made between generations simply by learning about the peculiarities of Clark Field, the Bossards, Maury Wills, Bill Bradley as a player and not a statesman, famous old stadiums and arenas, and the other stories collected in these pages.

The authors hope you have fun with the content. Best wishes for the future and thanks for your interest.

THE TURF BATTLES IN MAJOR LEAGUE BASEBALL

| Credit: Shutterstock

WHO'S FERTILIZING AND WHO ISN'T

There are few standards that define what constitutes a surface on which sports are played. This is no different in baseball. The bases are required to be 90 feet apart, the pitching mound is 60 feet 6 inches from home plate, no more than 10 inches above the level of home plate, with specific rules on location, diameter, and slope [1]. What constitutes the field is quite a bit broader, as are its dimensions. Other than being level, base paths, while traditionally dirt, have flexible specifications for their compositions. Outfields and foul territories vary in size and shape, and their consistency is a wide variety of grass and artificial turf. The fact that both the home and away teams play on the same field at the same time is thought to be an equalizing factor in Major League Baseball (MLB), but historical observations have shown that player familiarity with their home ballpark and its composition can provide selective advantages.

There are two types of natural surfaces common with MLB teams: Kentucky bluegrass and Bermuda grass. Midwestern cities and those in the northeast typically use Kentucky bluegrass fields, while southern and western cities have more Bermuda grass. Bermuda tends to be more drought resistant and grows more extensively in hotter climates, so it's not surprising to find it more common in baseball fields in warmer sites.

In additional to Kentucky bluegrass and Bermuda grass, Tampa and Toronto have synthetic turf surfaces and Miami and Houston have seashore paspalum grass surfaces. Tropicana Field in Tampa is generally hated by both the players and the management in Tampa. The team has contracted to install at least five different artificial turf surfaces since they arrived in 1997 [2], including changes in 2017 and 2018. The Rays have outlined their plans to vacate Tropicana for a better stadium with a natural turf surface by 2023 at the earliest, and they need to resolve the funding for a new, nearly $1B stadium. In the meantime, the Rays are stuck at Tropicana with their ever-changing playing surface. Everybody else in this group looks to be stable in their current confines.

Again, Bermuda grass tends to be more common in southern and drought prone climates while Bluegrass is found on fields in northern climates. Bermuda grass is a wiry and spongy turf surface that's viable only from climate zones 7-10 in the United States. The resilience of the grass is attributed to the integrity of the wiry stems of the plants which grow the grass. The wire meshwork of the turf recovers quickly making

Bermuda grass a desirable surface for high traffic areas. Moderate to high amounts of watering and frequent mowings yield the most robust Bermuda surfaces.

Bluegrass tends to germinate in single blades below the soil. The individual blades are very soft making it pleasant to walk on. The texture can vary a little, but the blades are rather fine and easily bent under mechanical loading. Bluegrass tends to wilt under excessive wear conditions, but its saving grace is that it grows extensively in cold weather climates, hence the popularity in northern climate baseball fields.

The real tests between turf surfaces can be conducted when a team opts for a new type of blade. The Philadelphia Phillies opted to yank out their Bermuda grass infield for Bluegrass in 2016 thanks to Philadelphia's manager Larry Bowa (more on him later). The rationale was that the Bermuda grass was so spongy that balls hit the grass surface and bounced like it was AstroTurf. The move to create a more absorbent surface was based on a team goal to favor defense and use ground ball pitchers. As expected, after the bluegrass surface was installed, players on the Phillies found that balls going through the infield were slowed [21]. For the right pitchers, this switch could lower earned run averages. In fact, after the change, the Phillies team ERA dropped from 4.63 (2016) to 4.55 (2017) to 4.14 (2018) [20].

There are a couple of hybrid stadiums where the infield and outfield are different (Arizona), or a blend of grasses (Philadelphia), where the infield is Bluegrass and outfield is Bermuda grass. Cincinnati is another outlier by using rye grass. Regardless of the surface, groundskeepers are commissioned across the continent to make their fields flourish, but baseball played in one city on one surface can be quite different than the baseball played in another city.

WHY DON'T YOU SEE WEEDS AT YOUR LOCAL BALLPARK?

It's simple. While most of us homeowners are part time groundskeepers around the house, each team hires an army of turf specialists and groundskeepers to pick every weed that would germinate on the field.

In addition, the actual fields are designed for limited access and are rarely used for anything other than baseball, so there are fewer concerns that the field might be compromised.

Turf management is the realm of the agricultural schools and universities that are graduating crops of agronomists and plant growers that end up working for seed and fertilizer companies. They focus on methods such as enhanced soil aeration, top dressing, irrigation, drainage, and strategies to increase overall grass health. MLB does agronomy on a larger scale than any individual does at home.

There are legions of groundskeepers who aim to maintain the high quality of turf standards at professional fields, some who grew up in the business while others have been schooled. One can't talk about groundskeepers without talking with reverence about the Bossard family (more on them later also) who've set the standard for turf maintenance in Major League Baseball and beyond.

OPTIMIZE YOUR TEAM BASED ON YOUR TURF

Just for fun, let us assume you're an MLB team Owner. After finding, building, or otherwise appropriating a stadium of satisfactory dimensions, the next issue to consider is your players. An analytics question (think "*Moneyball*") is whether a single player, assuming he (and maybe she) could play for several different teams, would be more successful playing in one location over the others considering weather and field composition alone.

Do the Colorado Rockies look for players who can hit home runs in rarified air? Do the Minnesota Twins look for players who are unafraid of defending solid ball contact (high "ball exit speed") during cold days in April? Do the Tampa Rays look for players with good knees [2, 3] who can play on AstroTurf indefinitely or can field high ground balls due to the coefficient of restitution of a rubberized AstroTurf? What happens when your team is aging on the field and you're locked into long-term contracts with the players? Can you manipulate the playing surface to help your team stay competitive? Is it even ethical to manipulate it [4]?

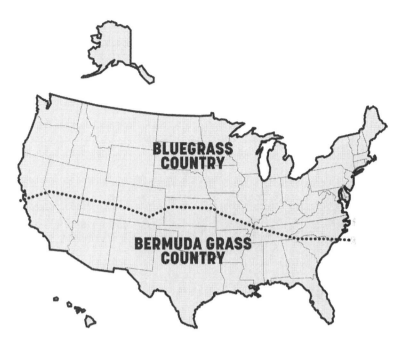

Northern climates have varieties of Bluegrass and southern parks tend to have Bermuda.

Broadly defined, that correlation between establishing the composition of the home team and winning in the scope of home field advantage and it has been assessed repeatedly by sports statisticians [5]. Perhaps that familiarity and comfort with playing at home and sleeping in one's own bed makes one more apt to play better. Perhaps the fact that one is playing at home means that there are more fans of the home team to watch and cheer. Perhaps the umpires are intimidated and less likely to make a controversial call against the home team. With instant replay, it's less likely that judgment calls are as influenced by the home team crows, as in years past. For whatever reason, home field advantage is a real phenomenon.

From 2008-2010, Jon Bois at SB Nation tracked the performance stats for the 30 teams in MLB and found that all teams would play better if they had the chance to play the 81 seasonal away games at home instead [6]. The estimated gain in win percentage ranged from

3% (Los Angeles Angels and Miami Marlins) to ~10% (Pittsburgh Pirates and Detroit Tigers) with everyone else was in between. In other words, if Pittsburgh played 81 more games at home each year, they would average ~8 more wins per year and Miami would average ~2 more wins per year. Looking into different major American sports, Bois showed that the NBA had a larger home field advantage (10% more wins) than the NFL (6.4%) MLB (5.5%) and the NHL (5.3%) (Bois's team-specific data for the MLB is shown in Figure 2 [6]).

A deeper dive into whether there remains a home field advantage in the playoffs when the better teams are still competing suggests that, at least in baseball, the home field advantage is smaller (51% bias for the home team) than in the NBA (73%) [7].

HISTORICAL LOOKS AT HOW YOU CAN USE THE FIELD TO THE HOME TEAM'S ADVANTAGE

The Bossards in Cleveland, Chicago, and San Diego:

To date, three generations of the Bossard family have ruled over the fields linked with MLB teams in several cities including both the original and the newfangled Comiskey Park in Chicago, home to the White Sox. The family's influence on MLB has extended across the nation for over 100 years.

Great-Grandpa Emil Bossard was the head groundskeeper as early as 1911 with the minor league St. Paul Saints at Lexington Park in St. Paul, Minnesota, and after that with the Cleveland Indians starting in 1936. When he joined the Indians, Emil's sons Eugene, Harold, and Marshall all became Emil's de facto assistants. From there, the family proved spectacularly resourceful and loyal to the Indians and a grateful Lou Boudreau (player/manager for the Indians).

Eugene proved to be so good that the White Sox hired him away from Cleveland. The legacy continued in Eugene's son Roger, who took his father's place as the head groundskeeper at Comiskey—where he still works today. Roger Bossard has been innovative in turf management, drainage, and overall living turf quality. To give you some idea of the lure of the Bossard family, the White Sox drafted Roger's son, Brandon, in the 31st round 2016 MLB draft, probably in part to keep him from signing somewhere else and giving away all of Dad's secrets [22].

Roger Bossard "bobblehead."

The Bossard family is a legend not only for how to make grass grow, but they saw limitless potential in investing in every conceivable method to extract a perceived advantage. In his book *"The Cheater's Guide to Baseball,"* Derek Zumsteg explains in great detail the depths to which Cleveland was using data analytics on the field 70 years ago [8]. Clancy Sigal mentions in his article that Bossard and his two sons, Harold and Marshall, made "adjustments to the playing surface for each home game based on what they knew of the other teams tendencies and the Indian's likely lineup" [9].

It was breathtaking to see how in 1948, prior life experiences helped the Indians steal signs from the opposing catcher in an elaborate scheme, executed by Boudreau, and including both the groundskeepers and several Hall of fame pitchers with the Indians. Bob Feller had been a gunnery officer on board a Navy ship in WW II and used a telescope for spotting targets [10]. The telescope was about three feet long, but with good optics, and the spotter could see 100+ yards. After Feller's discharge, he came home with the telescope. The telescope made its way to Cleveland's scoreboard where Feller, or Bob Lemon, would sit and relay signs to Marshall or Harold Bossard, who were poking their heads through holes in the scoreboard where out-of-town scores were normally displayed [10]. They relayed signs day-by-day, changing from a face in the hole, to an arm hanging out, to a light flashing. The signs were signaled by the opposing catcher, interpreted by Bob Lemon or

Bob Feller, relayed to one of the Bossards, who would then relay the sign to the batter—all in a matter of seconds. Pretty sneaky.

Harold Bossard took over for his Dad, Emil, as head groundskeeper for the Indians in 1956. He continued the legend of the Bossards for another 21 years before retiring in 1977 [11]. Harold seemed to have the Bossard knack for storytelling and having fun. For the journalists covering the game, that was often an important feature. After Harold retired in 1977 from tending to the turf for both the Indians and the Cleveland Browns, Harold's son Brian, who studied agronomy at Purdue, took over as head groundskeeper for the football Browns until the San Diego Padres came calling in 1985 [11]. The Padres presented Brian with over 130 newspaper articles identifying all sorts of problems with the turf at Jack Murphy stadium in San Diego, a big challenge and probably one linked with a better salary and better weather for sure. Brian Bossard tore out the rocks underneath the infield turf at Jack Murphy stadium and replaced them with clay. Within three years Brian turned San Diego's infield at Jack Murphy into arguably the best field in the National League. Sadly, Brian passed away rather prematurely only eight years after heading to San Diego [12].

Eugene "Geno" Bossard, Harold's brother, who was born in 1918, was the one who left the flock and joined the White Sox in 1940 as head groundskeeper after his apprenticeship with dad and his brothers in Cleveland. Eugene took over at the ripe old age of 22. He was known for soaking the infield at Comiskey in Chicago so much that ground balls were significantly slowed as a result. Geno was a legend, having found a way to create a swamp-like condition to deaden the first bounce from a hard ground ball by digging up the ground around home plate, affectionately called Bossard's Swamp [13]. Eugene and his son Roger would be up very early in the morning or gameday, armed with hoses and pick-axes to soften things up. It was obvious to the players on both teams taking batting practice that hard ground balls hitting the muck would ricochet off globs of wet mud, but they played on.

Geno Bossard was probably singlehandedly the reason that a rag-tag group of White Sox with an average batting average of .225 and no batter higher than .241 could be competitive enough to be tied for the division lead as late in the season as September 6 in 1967 [14]. Eugene stayed for 40 years with the White Sox, ultimately retiring once Geno's son, Roger was ready to take over. Geno continued to help Roger with the field work at Comiskey until he died in 1998 at 80.

Like Brian Bossard, Roger also went to Purdue to study agronomy coupled with all of his practical training from his apprenticeship with Geno. He was destined for great things [14]. Roger officially joined the White Sox as a groundskeeper in 1967 and took over for Geno as head groundskeeper in 1983. What Roger learned at Purdue he put into practice in Chicago, developing a more functional drainage system which was ultimately patented for wider use. Other teams and the league took notice and worked with Roger directly to develop more functional drainage systems to reduce the number of rainouts. Roger's patented sand-based drainage systems are now found in 19 MLB and minor league parks [15]. The venues include both Chicago locations, Detroit, Milwaukee, St Louis, Boston, New York, San Diego, Seattle Arizona, and Washington D.C. [16]. This notoriety birthed the nickname "the Sodfather" and Roger has his own wiki site [16]. Heck, even the White Sox had a bobblehead night for the head groundskeeper—where does that happen other than in Chicago [16]?

ACROSS TOWN: THE CHICAGO CUBS

Across town from Comiskey Park during the 1984 season, the Cubs were stocked with great pitchers like Rick Sutcliffe, Dennis Eckersley, Steve Trout and Scott Sanderson, and won their division but lost in the divisional playoffs. Most of the starters were quite good at coaxing ground balls out of the opposing team and there was a lot of activity in the infield during the 1984 season. Embarking on another year in 1985, the team had a second baseman in Ryne Sandberg who was just coming into his own as a terrific infielder, but on the left side of the diamond saw Ron Cey at third base and Larry Bowa at shortstop—both great infielders in their prime—but each had slowed considerably as both past their 35th birthdays.

Remember Bowa, the manager of the Phillies in 2016, when they were coerced into a new turf because the infielders couldn't respond to ground balls in time? In 1985, the Cubs, who were seeing grounders make it past their shortstop and third basemen in practice, came up with a practical solution—they would leave the grass long on the left side of infield to slow ground balls. UPI ran a story in mid-May during the 1985 season stating that the grass in Chicago was at least an inch taller than any other ballpark in MLB [17]. Al Bumbry, a reserve with the Padres at the time remarked that he didn't think the mowers actually had any blades as they traversed the field [17].

If you have pitchers who are producing ground balls, and the infielders are too slow to get them, the next best approach, if you're playing at home, is to slow the ball down by having ground balls bounce and roll through much thicker grass. While the Cubs had to also bat with the thick left side of the diamond, the management believed the team was more competitive when their defense was retiring ball players on ground balls. The ploy was obvious enough to rankle other Cubs players, who complained that they were grounding out more often as well with hits that would, in any other ballpark, find their way to left field.

Of course, the Cubs were doomed with this strategy, as the one thing they hadn't planned on was having their ground ball pitchers on the DL for much of the 1985 season, and when other pitchers that got the call were not getting ground balls, the height of the grass doesn't help. When the Cubs ultimately got a new shortstop with wider range, suddenly the grass was shorn much shorter [18]. The Cubs had enough other problems that addressing the grass height was not the panacea the brass had envisioned.

Brian is partial to the Cubs, who have had to maintain both the grass and the ivy [19] on the outfield wall, but he has a much better appreciation for what has happened on the other side of town. Of course, fast-forward 30+ years later and the Cubs finally put most of the curses to rest, winning the World Series in 2016.

FINALLY!

ALSO ACROSS TOWN

Soldier Field, home to the Chicago Bears, was built in preparation for the World's Fair in Chicago and is a legacy park just off Lake Michigan. The field is natural grass although the distinction between different bluegrasses important. Members of the Bears complained about the field being easily chewed up and slippery. Prior to the 2014 season in which Soldier Field switched from an Illinois-based sod producer to one from New Jersey [23], one would not expect one blue-grass versus another would have many differences, but the sod from New Jersey had more sand than clay as compared to the Illinois prod-uct. In this case, supporting sod farmers in Illinois ran counter to providing a better playing surface. Higher sand concentration main-tains the cohesive strength of the turf so that it doesn't get easily chewed up by cleats and appears less slippery when wet. If the Bears were winning in the bog of Soldier Field leading up to the turf change, perhaps management would have made a different decision, but the switch they made was ultimately safer for the players and the referees alike.

Creative engineered solutions about turf surfaces are forthcoming. Supple grass fields have been produced, even within dome structures like the one at the University of Phoenix's "State Farm Stadium" where the Arizona Cardinals play. This structure is designed to shield the grass from the oppressive desert heat by having the turf on a rolling track that they can roll into the dome [24]. This required a separate space at the field level adjacent to the dome to which the field is wheeled when not in use. In this manner, turf managers are able to produce a schedule of sun exposure that is less stressful and allows the turf to thrive while shielding the most damaging effects of the Phoenix climate.

Despite their efforts, this playing surface has had some issues for the players. In December 2018, the Detroit Lions beat the Cardinals in Arizona and complained bitterly that the field was being torn up in clumps and players were sliding all over the place. Eight different Lions went down with injuries during the game. Ricky Jean Francois, a Lions defensive lineman, told *Detroit Free Press* reporters that "You pay too much money for a stadium like this to have grass that bad. I'm just saying, if you're going to spend billions (on the stadium) you might as well cover everything." [25]

Overall, give due to the groundskeepers who work diligently to maintain natural turf field surfaces. While their efforts largely go unnoticed, surfaces clearly play a critical role in professional sports and can affect the competitiveness of your favorite team.

MAURY WILLS AND THE 1962 MLB SEASON

Stopping the Greatest Base Stealer of All Time

M aury Wills was an exceptional major league baseball player, serving primarily as a shortstop for the Los Angeles Dodgers in the 1960s. Wills earned numerous MLB honors, including National League MVP (1962), two Gold Gloves (1961, 1962), seven All Star selections, and three World Series Championships. Alongside his accolades, Wills is best known for stealing bases.

Wills was a prominent base runner, leading the National League in stolen bases for six consecutive seasons. He had an exceptional work ethic, was speedy, and was determined to be the best. When on base, Wills was as gifted at stealing a base as anyone who'd ever played the game. His constant threat to steal continuously affected the game for opposing pitchers.

There's only so much that can be done to counteract a player of Wills' abilities. Really good battery combinations and skilled pick-off attempts have proven to be successful at keeping runners from advancing from stolen bases. There are certain calls that aid in defense of stolen bases, such as pitchouts and throwing fastballs to the hitter so that the catcher receives the ball incrementally faster than with an off-speed pitch such as a curveball or a knuckler. These tactics didn't seem to make a difference for Maury Wills in 1962.

LOSING TRACTION: THE ONLY WAY TO STOP MAURY WILLS

Noel Hynd at *Sports Illustrated* tells a great story [1]. Flashback to August 10-12, 1962 where the San Francisco Giants are in second place in the National League, a few games back from the Los Angeles Dodgers. The Dodgers had a roster stacked with superstars like pitchers Sandy Koufax, Don Drysdale, and Maury Wills—who would break Ty Cobb's record of 104 stolen bases that season. Wills was simply more talented a base stealer than anyone could effectively keep in check on the base paths. It just wasn't fair when he got on base.

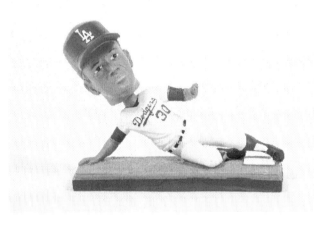

| Maury Willis "bobblehead."

As the Dodgers arrived at Candlestick Park, home of the Giants, countermeasures were being developed specifically to contain Wills. In the dark of night before the first game of the series, head groundskeeper Matthew (Matty) Schwab and his son Jerry dug up the first base path around where Wills would stand, ready to steal bases against the hometown Giants. The Schwabs were also legends in the groundskeeping business and the only reason Matty was available was that San Francisco lured him away when Branch Rickey, GM of the Brooklyn Dodgers and a known skinflint, refused to give the groundskeeper a raise when he was in charge at Ebbets Field[2]. Matty and Jerry dug up the topsoil in the turf and in its place, put a loose mixture of wet sand and peat moss. The top inch of that 5x15-foot first-base area was covered with the original soil to hide evidence of the doctored field surface.

It was obvious to the Dodgers, once they arrived at Candlestick, that the area around first base was sloppier and looser than near third. The Dodgers complained bitterly to the umpires who found the grounds crew and gave the Giants an ultimatum—fix the field or forfeit. Out came the shovels and wheelbarrows to remove the sticky concoction, only to be mixed with a little more dirt and carried back out onto the field again. It was as loose or looser than what was originally put on the field.

Wills went 1-4 in that first game without a stolen base attempt. In fact, the Dodgers as a team didn't attempt a single stolen base the entire game! With their speed neutralized, there wasn't much else the Dodgers could do, and they promptly lost 11-2.

Before game two, the San Francisco grounds crew dug up all of the evidence and replaced it with the original topsoil so that the league office, when tasked with checking for chicanery at Candlestick's turf, found no evidence of significant wrongdoing. For game two, the soil was still loose from digging, and thanks to the groundskeepers who liberally watered it, the path between first and second base was a muddy marshland.

As Danny Ostler on SFGate.com mentioned, the groundscrew watered the first base side like they were rice farmers[3]. It was so wet in fact that the umpires had to intervene midgame and again demand turf repairs. The Dodgers were so consumed with the question of what to do if they got on base that they struggled to make steals happen at all. In the end, the Dodgers were swept in the three-game series, recording just a single stolen base on two attempts across all three games, much lower than the 1.2 steals on 1.5 attempts per game the Dodgers averaged over the 1962 season (baseball-reference.com).

THE REMATCH

At the end of the 1962 season, the Giants and Dodgers tied for the league pennant, triggering a three-game playoff with games one and three in San Francisco and game two in L.A. Sure enough, plans were made in San Francisco to replicate the field conditions that shut down the Dodger base stealers in August. But the umpires were already on site, prepped to be on the lookout for anything unusual. Conditions were better for stealing in that series. Maury Wills went 4-for-4 in stolen base attempts (recording record-setting stolen bases #101, 102, 103, and 104) but it wasn't enough, and the Giants prevailed to capture the NL pennant. While the giants went on to lose the 1962 World Series, four games to three to the New York Yankees, one has to wonder how much the August series played a role in keeping the Dodgers from the postseason.

While Wills's single-season base-running record was eventually broken (the modern-day record belongs to Rickey Henderson who stole 130 bases in 1982 for the Oakland Athletics), BaseballReference.com credits Maury Wills' 1962 104-steal season as the most runs generated from an individual player's base stealing in MLB history (19), which shows, even more, why slowing Wills down, even in just a three-game series, was such a critical outcome for the San Francisco Giants.

BAD ICE

How NHL Teams Keep Their Ice Frozen

| Credit: Shutterstock

A way of leveling competition between two unequal opponents is to change the field conditions on which the opponents are competing. Hockey is played on an imperfect surface and, in many ways, changing the ice surface probably impacts the play in hockey more than any other sport. Say a hockey team isn't particularly fast or skilled at puck handling and they're up against a team stacked with swift skaters and deft stick handlers. If the ice is sufficiently rutty, such that the sliding the puck or the skate is fraught with more friction and less glide, the difficulty in skating could even out the difference in skill and speed between the two opponents. Thus, lower ice quality could make for an ugly low-scoring game by making goals more random and the game less about finesse and skill.

CONTROLLING ICE QUALITY

It seems relatively easy to make poor ice. Most everyone in the north has seen flooded backyards where amateurs have made their own ice rinks in the winter. That's about as uncontrolled as it gets. The process of making ice in an NHL rink is far more involved. Inherent variables include initial water quality and composition, humidity, the freeze rate of the ice layers, and the precision by which the ice is built.

It takes approximately four days to build a sheet of ice from scratch, according to Brandon Klein of Wired.com. The water to make ice is typically a brine solution, which is first purified of other solutes and run through reverse osmosis to remove trace minerals and dissolved oxygen. The final saltwater solution is sprayed onto a layer of concrete suspended over a heat exchange/chiller system, much like in your refrigerator. When the brine is sprayed out, the coils in the heat exchange continuously extract heat from above and the brine rapidly freezes without equilibrating to the air in the arena.

The first layers are poured or sprayed out so that there is an adequate base of frigid ice. Once the ice is approximately ½ to 1 inch thick, the Zamboni resurfacing vehicles come out to scrape out irregularities on the ice surface and deposit a thin layer of new ice. Typically, the ice surface is about 0.03 inches thicker with each subsequent pass. Resurfacings are important at each intermission. Without them, referees would be constantly patching holes as ruts and grooves grow over the course of a game.

Ice is frustrating to freeze. There's a sizable amount of air dissolved in water at ambient temperature and without these extensive measures, a lot of dissolved oxygen would remain in the ice as it freezes. Air is more soluble in warmer water and as the water temperature lowers and ice forms, air is expelled and often trapped as little voids, making the white air-filled pocket typically seen in the center of common ice cubes. Ice is lower in density than the water it comes from and is more buoyant due to the air bubbles sealed within. Ice is more translucent, yet most NHL rinks are typically lustrous and clear, which comes from fewer air inclusions due to more control of both the brine and the rapidity of the freezing. It's more than the look that's important, as ice with air pockets will also chip easier and become ruddy more quickly.

ICE DIFFERENCES IN THE NHL

In 2017, there was a bundle of problems at a variety of arenas concerning ice quality. Rinks in Arizona, Edmonton, Carolina, Detroit, and Brooklyn were singled out for non-NHL quality ice[1]. If we know how to make good ice, why is it that some venues garner reputations for lousy ice? One reason could be that some systems for producing ice aren't as good as others. Some legacy rinks were built in the 1920s. The oldest current NHL surface dates back to the late 1990s.

Refrigeration technologies have advanced sufficiently so that the difference between a rink built in 1995 and one built this year isn't as dramatic as one from 1930. Another reason for the challenges is that different geographical locations put a different strain on HVAC (Heating, Ventilation, and Air Conditioning) systems in the building and for the ice. It's a lot easier to build and maintain a rink in the cold climate of Fairbanks, Alaska than one in the dry heat of Arizona.

Another environmental factor affecting ice surfaces is the humidity created by spectators. Hockey is a spectator sport, and if there are 15,000 sets of lungs exhaling moist humid air for several hours, the arena humidity can rise substantially and higher humidity equilibrates with the outside layers of ice [2]. Humidity in hockey arenas rises to as much as 50-60% by the end of a game. Leave it to hockey-loving Ontarians to measure something like that [3]. The humid air dissolves into the outside layers of the ice, and those layers, which have the highest humidity, are most susceptible to chipping. These susceptible layers will be softer than the lower surfaces of chilled ice, creating an uneven playing surface. Not to say a completely dehumidified surface is good either. Extremely low humidity can also cause the ice to be brittle and fracture. There's a fine balance to humidity and the ice rink.

It would be one thing if the ice remained idle when there weren't practices or games. If it did, it would make arenas pretty expensive to maintain and operate with only game days paying the ice bills. For that reason, many rinks are dual or triple use facilities with basketball, concerts, conventions, and various forms of entertainment activities (like circuses) squeezing in when the team isn't playing. These activities require alternative surfaces to be laid over the ice. Each time the arena is filled, it's another chance for 15,000 sets of lungs to produce hot, moist, and humid air, requiring repair to the ice below. There are currently 11 NHL teams that share their facility with another team. Those 11 arenas are likely to have more humidity exposure than single-use rinks.

POOR ICE CONDITIONS

If a compressor fails and the chillers cannot produce, games can't be played. Poor conditions have led to the cancellation of NHL games in the past. In 2017, a preseason game in Arizona was canceled due to poor ice conditions following a Saturday night concert at the same arena(4).

More often, teams play through poor conditions. On May 20, 1975 in game three of the Stanley Cup Finals, the Buffalo Sabres hosted the Philadelphia Flyers in what would be known as the "Fog Game [5]." Memorial Auditorium in Buffalo was built in 1940 and renovated in 1970 for the NHL expansion Sabres. The Sabres didn't make the playoffs until the 1974-75 season and weren't used to playing that late in the NHL season. Temperatures reached 27 degrees C (80.6 F) in Buffalo that day and it was even hotter in the arena where 15,000+ packed inside without air conditioning. The ice started melting, creating fog. Whole players disappeared into the mist. The game was stopped five times in regulation and another seven in overtime due to the conditions. Buffalo won the game 5-4 in overtime with the Flyers' goalie, Bernie Parent, claiming to have never seen the puck that clinched it for the Sabres. The Flyers ultimately won the series in six games.

Players will sometimes comment critically on how the ice affected games. The open question is: do teams ever deliberately make bad ice? There have been instances where bad ice has affected the outcome of games. In the middle of the 2016-17 NHL season, Arizona was playing on the road against the New York Islanders. The Coyotes had some really good skaters and Cal Clutterbuck, playing for the Islanders, commented that the low quality of the ice slowed down some of the young speedy forwards on the Arizona team. The Islanders went on to scratch out a 3-2 win and Clutterbuck claimed that the ice was the worst he'd ever played on in the NHL [4]. The issue with the Barclays Center seems to be a structural one where PVC piping is used for some of the cooling systems under the ice which apparently is essentially sub-standard for the NHL [8]. The humidity is a sufficiently identified problem at Barclays that a gaggle of dehumidifiers was used to help take humidity out of the building in advance of play during the warmer playoff season in the spring[8]. If it's a structural problem with the production of inferior ice, its likely to happen more often than not, but it was one that paid off that night for the Islanders. One wonders if poor ice conditions could change the desired makeup of a hockey team. Teams with newer, less humidity-challenged facilities could recruit gliders and finesse players. Poor conditioned ice goes to sturdy grinders and possession players.

Hockey games played outdoors pose an even greater problem for ice quality. The Winter Classic has become a yearly tradition in the NHL. In the inaugural game on January 1st, 2008 at Ralph Wilson Stadium Orchard Park, NY (home to the Buffalo Bills), snow fell and blizzard conditions ensued. The ice surface was covered in snow, making skating and puck movement challenging. Frequent shoveling temporarily cleared the snow, but the weather persisted. The conditions did make for an iconic ending as Sidney Crosby won the game in the shootout, pushing the puck through a snow-covered surface amidst falling flakes [7].

THE DECREASING INFLUENCE OF HOCKEY HOME ICE ADVANTAGE

The National Hockey League has undergone significant expansion since its early days. Including the Original Six that predate 1967 (Toronto, Montreal, Chicago, Detroit, New York, and Boston), there are now 31 teams in the league, including teams in hot climates like the Anaheim Mighty Ducks, Florida Panthers, Phoenix Coyotes, San Jose Sharks, Dallas Stars, and the latest expansion Las Vegas Golden Knights.

One of the features of the original NHL were indoor arenas that predated anything with standard dimensions. There were NHL league standards for new hockey rinks, but the original facilities were mostly unmodified during the initial league expansion. It was only after substantial league expansion that the league was able to demand rink dimensions be standardized across the entire NHL, which didn't happen until 1999.

THE ORIGINAL SIX AND OLD RINKS

The current standards for an NHL rink are 200 feet in length and 85 feet in width. There's a defined radius of curvature linked with the corners of each rink. Every NHL playing surface has to be built to these standards. Further rules define the dimensions of the crease, neutral zone, face-off locations, penalty box and bench locations. During the heyday of the Original Six, only New York and Montreal had rinks of the same dimensions. Toronto's Maple Leaf Gardens had standard area dimensions, but the corners were more rounded than those in New York or Montreal. Detroit's Olympia Stadium was two feet more narrow in width, and Boston (191 x 83) and Chicago (188 x 85) were relatively short in length[1].

Expansion in 1967 welcomed six new teams to the NHL (the Los Angeles Kings, California Golden Seals, Philadelphia Flyers, Pittsburgh Penguins, St Louis Blues, and Minnesota North Stars). Two more teams joined in 1970 (the Buffalo Sabres and Vancouver Canucks). With the exception of Buffalo, these new teams played in rinks of standard size. Buffalo's arena was even shorter than the rink in Chicago at 185 feet in length [2].

Tony McKegney, who played for the Sabres, mentioned that playing on the short Buffalo rink ended up being a real advantage for them [2]. The distance between blue lines was smaller and passing between players required more technical focus to avoid offsides calls. The visiting teams had a more abrupt adjustment, but the team in Buffalo was used to playing cramped on the short rink. Skating in Buffalo's crowded rink meant that technically the team was prepared when it came to playing at larger rinks like Montreal.

St Nicholas Skating Rink, an early hockey venue in New York, 1896-1897. *Credit: Tom Barrow, hockeygods.com.*

There's little doubt that pre-standardized rinks gave an advantage to home teams. Swartz et al. highlighted a drop in home ice advantage from 1979 to 2011. This paper showed a decline in the home team winning percentage from ∼ 60% times to ∼ 55% [3]. Their findings also showed the home team scored on average 0.3 more goals per game than their visiting opponent, down from approximately 0.7 in 1979, which is a decreased goal differential of 57%. Using the NBA as a comparison (another fast-paced and team scoring sport) the data showed the decline in home ice advantage was more dramatic than home court advantage of the NBA, which was also declining. Another analysis comparing major sports in the United States showed current home ice advantage to be several percentages lower than NBA (which is still nearly 60% home wins) and the NFL (nearly 57% home wins), according to Curtis Stock of the Edmonton Journal [4].

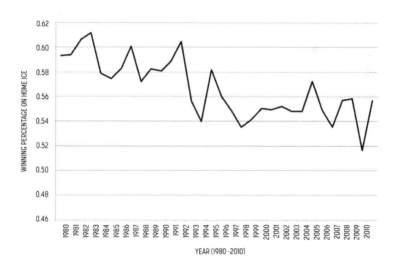

"New Insights Involving the Home Team Advantage." Tim Sartz and Adriano Arce. *Credit: International Journal of Sport Science Coaching (2014), 9 (4), 681-692.*

LAST SHIFT CHANGES AND LUXURY BOXES

Beyond rink standardization, another feature of home-ice advantage is the last shift change rule. Rule 82-1 in the NHL handbook says, "Following the stoppage of play, the visiting team shall promptly place a line-up on the ice ready for play and no substitution shall be made from that time until play has been resumed. The home team may then make any desired substitution, except in cases following an icing, which does not result in the delay of the game" [5].

When playing at home, the visiting team has to put their team on the ice first, allowing the home team to organize their opposing group of players to neutralize an advantage or to leverage a perceived potential disadvantage. Ultimately, the opposing team has to get on the ice first and the home team responds. Several years back (2013), when legacy teams Boston and Toronto met in Boston, the coach for the Bruins always played his top defense team including Zdeno Chara and Dennis Seidenberg, whenever the Leaf's star wing Phil Kessel went into play [6]. These two Bruins defensemen seemed more effective at neutralizing Kessel than his other defensive pairings and, therefore, those matchups happened in Boston and maybe to a lesser extent in Toronto. If the same two teams played in Toronto, other disparities could be leveraged accordingly.

The culture of being at a hockey rink has evolved as well. The proliferation of skyboxes has pushed arguably some of the biggest hockey fans into the skyboxes well above the rink level action. The general perception is that the current hockey culture works in certain locations where fans feel involved, and less so in others where fans feel isolated from the game. The Nashville Predators were an extremely competitive team in the mid-2010s and the perception was that the fans were active components of the rink's atmosphere, making their home (Bridgestone Arena) a challenging place to play and win as a road team [7]. Before the Predators caught fire with their base, the team was not financially viable and was considering relocating. Home fan engagement and participation is not a new revelation as perennial Stanley Cup contenders such as Detroit and Pittsburgh often have a rabid fan base that can present a playoff atmosphere and challenge to visiting opponents. There's no question that hockey arenas are loud, between few natural sound absorbers among the building materials including the boards, the ceiling, seats, etc., and loud PA and music systems. In 2010, during the playoffs between the Blackhawks and Philadelphia Flyers, the noise level peaked at ∼115 dB in Philadelphia and ∼120 dB in Chicago, comparable to a rock concert, but probably close enough to be statistically insignificant between venues [8].

Rob Vollman did an incredible deep dive that found that the NHL rulebook also provides other perceived advantages for the home team [9]. When at home, the home team gets to go the locker room first after each period, supplies the game pucks, selects which side of the ice to play on longer, gets more advantageous face off sites if the location for the infraction is ambiguous, and gets the decide who shoots first in a shoot out if the score is tied at the end of the game [9]. It's not possible to completely resolve whether any of these slight tilts have any overall difference on home team performance, but it's interesting to consider.

Maybe home ice is a bigger advantage once a team gets to the playoffs. Fundamentally, there's more parity between teams once the weaker teams don't extend into the playoffs [10]. At least that was the thinking in 2018 when very few home teams lost during first rounds of the NHL playoffs.

Far from the early days of custom rinks, home ice advantage is being lost with standardization of ice surfaces and redistribution of rabid fans into more widely distributed open venues. These features can make fans more spectators or observers, rather than active participants in the action. Projecting into the future, as pervasive engagement in mobile phones and social media, more emphasis on specialized concessions and entertainment (such as legalized fantasy and team sports gambling) suggests that fewer and fewer fans will actually watch what is occurring rinkside, leveling the advantage of home ice even more.

CLAY COURTS AND THE FRENCH OPEN

Domination by Nadal, difficulty for others

| Groundskeeper raking a Hartru court.

The French Open is a major tennis tournament played annually in late May and early June on the outskirts of Paris. As a visiting American tennis fan, it is a chance to find a French bistro that makes entrecôte beef steak and pommes frites. It's a chance to sample real baguettes and croissants, Orangina in a can, crêpes avec sucre et limon, and enjoy springtime in Paris. As a tennis-playing American professional, it hasn't proven to be such an enjoyable trip. Americans have struggled mightily in this tournament. The cause is likely from a combination of play style and conditions.

AMERICAN WOES AT THE FRENCH OPEN

Other than Serena Williams, no American man or woman has won the French Open since 1999[1]. Serena, with 23 career Grand Slam singles titles, has won the French Open three times. She attributes her success, in part, because she likes to slide on the French Open's clay surfaces. While in a class of her own, Serena has struggled at the French relative to the other three Grand Slam Tournaments. Serena has won three of the 16 French open tournaments she has participated in (18.8%)— significantly lower than her success at the other three grand slam tournaments. Serena has dominated the Australian Open in seven of 17 attempts (41.2%), Wimbledon in seven of 18 tries (38.9%), and the U.S. Open in six of 18 tournaments (33.3%). Additionally, her singles win percentage at the French Open is 5% lower than any of the other three, suggesting she is underperforming at the French relative to the other venues.

On the men's side, it's even worse. You say to yourself, no way... John McEnroe, Jimmy Connors, Arthur Ashe, and Pete Sampras...one of these guys had to have won this thing at least once. And you'd be wrong.

This is the single championship holding these men up from a career grand slam. Since the late 1960s, only Andre Agassi, Michael Chang and Jim Courier (twice) have won the French Open [1]. While Americans comprise 10% of the top 100 players on both the women's and men's sides, U.S. men have won the French sparingly. With this large a portion of top players being American, the likelihood that one would win a championship seems higher than that.

Considering the men's side for the period from 1960-2018 (59 years) there have been 14 (23.7%) American winners of the Australian Open, 16 (27.1%) for Wimbledon, 19 (32.2%) for the US Open, and only four (6.8%) for the French Open. Why is the French Open at Roland Garros so challenging?

THE CHALLENGE OF CLAY COURTS

The French Open is the only major tournament played on red clay. Tennis played on red clay tends to increase the amount of rebound a ball has, while slowing it relative to other surfaces[2]. The slower ball and the larger bounce allow players to reach for balls that would otherwise go unreturned. A new pattern of footwork is required on clay as players tend to slide more on the bottoms of their soles, thus there's less running and more sliding into place and it takes time to be comfortable performing this action. Clay courts also tend to be more forgiving on joints, and athletes who play mostly on clay tend to have longer careers than those banging away on asphalt surfaces. There aren't statistics to indicate exactly how many clay courts there are in the U.S. relative to other places, but within the United States, estimates are that 10% of all courts are clay and only 1-in-100 of those clay courts are red clay.

Not all clay courts are the same. To understand the differences we need to look at geology. The most common clay courts are produced from red or green clays. The clays have different colors due to mineral content and red and green are dramatically different surfaces when crushed and left to the elements. Within the U.S., green clay is made of Precambrian metamorphic rocks called metabasalts, found in the Blue Ridge Mountains in what is called the Greenville Province—a long strip of mined green basalt rocks. There are many other places where this type of rock is found, including the Catoctin formation near the Catoctin Mountains in Maryland and Virginia, and other areas along the blue ridge[3]. These rocks can be crushed, ground, and spread to create a clayish surface. These basaltic rocks are rather hygroscopic and tend to soak up water during rains making these surfaces relatively durable and rapidly drying, allowing for rapid play after a storm. Green clay (also known as rubico or HarTru) surfaces tend to play more like asphalt with faster ball speed. While these courts do have some forgiving qualities, the rationale for using green over red clay is really based on performance and aesthetics. Green clay courts tend to be truer in terms of bounces, and are less prone to variations in texture given the peaks and valleys that are formed with continued play[4].

Balls tend to be easier to see while playing, as red clay tends to cling to tennis balls, and red clay courts absorb less light, making it more difficult to observe the ball vs. green clay courts[4].

Green clay courts are swept regularly to maintain their firmness and make traction more consistent. The need for maintenance has meant that most of these facilities are built in membership-fueled clubs. Most municipalities and schools lack discretionary money in their budgets to staff and maintain clay courts. Blow the leaves off with a blower, sure, but daily watering and sweeping, never. The U.S. National Tennis Center in Orlando has 32 green clay courts as opposed to six imported red clay courts[4].

Red clay courts have similar maintenance requirements and are expensive in the same way as the green clay courts, but there are important differences.

Red clay, found on many courts in Europe, is primarily produced from crushed limestone and bricks. Original clay courts were formed from ground-up clay pots and metered out on grass courts mainly to keep the grass from burning up during summers in the U.K. [5]. Clay is the preferred surface in much of Western Europe and Latin America due to its relatively low cost. Everyone in Europe and Latin America knows how to grab the rake and drag it around the court before playing. Calcium chloride is commonly added to retain water in red clays. Like green clay, while players are playing in the sun, the heat is baking the water out of the intended humid clay.

There's a pretty significant maintenance schedule tied to red clay, as the courts need to be raked, to break up agglomerates that can form after a rain. The largest issue with red clay courts is that if exposed to a significant rain event, particles of clay can be washed away, requiring new clay to be added to the surface. It's also sometimes challenging for clay courts to adequately drain, although improved designs are addressing this concern. New types of red clay surfaces at Roland Garros are layered structures built on 10-inch thick layers of stone, six inches of water permeable filtering slag, several inches of limestone, and only a few millimeters of clay silt layered on top of the composite surface[6]. This type of design allows water to drain more effectively through permeable gaps between the bricks. During the French Open, the courts are covered at night and watered in the morning along with a deposit of calcium chloride onto the clay surfaces to help them retain their water over the course of each playing day[6].

Red clay courts are being built in the U.S. with the intent of exposing developing players to the nuances of this surface. There are a handful of venues that have a limited number of red clay courts, but many of these are in leafy suburbs with posh tennis clubs catering to something other than the masses.

Interestingly, even as late as 2015, several courts at Roland Garros had a different construction as the clay was simply deposited on a concrete slab. This means that courts three, four, five, and the Suzanne Lenglen court all are more prone to drainage problems and thus, there's likely more urgency to cover these courts before those that drain more easily [6]. It also means that the random assignment or a match on one court or another may actually mean a different playing edge if playing in a well-draining court over one that retains water.

STRASBOURG, France: Groundskeeper waters a red clay tennis court, May 17th, 2017. *Credit: Shutterstock*

THE DOMINANCE OF RAFAEL NADAL–THE "KING OF CLAY"

One recent professional men's tennis player has completely dominated clay tennis. The "King of Clay" is Rafael (Rafa) Nadal of Spain, having won 11 of the past 14 French Opens (2005-2018)[7]. Having grown up on the Island of Mallorca, in the Mediterranean Sea east of Valencia, Rafa had his choice of clay courts to play on with a large number of tennis clubs on the island. Mallorca has a near-ideal climate for clay tennis—lots of sunshine, and not much rain. Rafa must have played a lot of tennis as a junior and his speed and athleticism have allowed him to be so dominant that he's won an astounding 92% of his matches on clay as opposed to 77% on all other surfaces [8]. He has exceptional footwork and endurance, allowing him to be quick and nimble on the sliding surface. Nadal's technique allow him to play exceptionally well on clay [9]. Nadal hits with powerful top-spin, making his returns difficult to control on a slow court.

| Credit: hartru.com

PRACTICE MAKES PERFECT

Revisiting the difficulty U.S. players have on clay courts, let's look at the training of U.S. players. Most of the court used to train elite American junior tennis players are smooth, well-constructed asphalt surfaces that emphasize certain playing skills. The traction required to play on hard courts might make someone a lethal player because of the consistency of balls being returned and bouncing on these well-groomed courts. But clay courts have ruts, grooves, bad bounces, and simply more random and chaotic responses to balls being bounced on them. The majority of available playing surfaces in the U.S. are made from asphalt, including those which junior players and collegians play on. Schools and municipalities who take it upon themselves to produce courts for their residents typically don't have the financing or staff required to maintain a more demanding surface such as clay. Ultimately, there are enough opportunities to successfully make a career out of playing on hard courts, that one doesn't have to learn how to play well on clay. Unless U.S.-based players invest in a larger schedule playing on clay courts, or unless a Rafael Nadal is born in the United States, there will only be a select number of players who can compete at an elite level on these foreign playing surfaces.

DO PAST WINNERS HAVE AN EDGE WHEN GOLF TOURNAMENTS ARE HELD AT A SINGLE COURSE?

| Credit: Shutterstock

Augusta National Golf Course, home to the Masters Tournament every April, is one of the most epic golf venues ever imagined and as iconic as perhaps only the Old Course at St Andrews and Pebble Beach in California. Originally conceived by Bobby Jones and designed by Alister MacKenzie, Augusta National Golf Course is the crown jewel of the PGA and steeped in the historical lore. Built on the tributaries of the Savannah River, the place is probably as well manicured and tended in April as any outdoor links course in the world. Augusta is ~7000 yards long (set up 400 yards longer recently) and has hosted an annual tournament since 1934—four years after Jones retired as an amateur. Brian has only been as far as the front gates because the course was overrun with gawkers like him, who only wanted to taste and smell a little of the mystique linked with the place.

THE MASTERS: A SWEET DEAL ALL AROUND

Augusta National is a special place. Membership initiation fees range around $20,000 and annual dues per member are ~$4,000 per year. Serial member users probably pay more, but in the end, the overall costs are reasonable [1]. The waiting list for new members is so long that there's no budget risk and the club makes so much money off of the Masters itself that it doesn't have to gouge its members or visitors who covet tickets for such an exclusive event.

For that $4,000 per year, members have to find another place to play from May through October when the groundskeepers work to on the course [2, 3] for the April tournament. The members are also likely not to be able to play much in March before the early April Master's weekend, as many tour players fly in to get an early look at how the course is set up. Of all of the major championships, only the Masters is played at the same venue year after year. It might suggest that members of the club or prior winners at Augusta might be more likely to win again on the same course if it suits their style of play.

The Masters is so important to the PGA that the PGA essentially hands the calendar to the organizers in Augusta and asks them which week they want the tournament to take place. From there, the rest of the schedule is filled in. This is why the azaleas are in peak season for each Masters. If global warming led to the azaleas blooming a week early, the PGA would pencil Augusta in earlier in their schedule. The tournament committee at Augusta negotiates a different deal in terms of broadcast coverage compared with the rest of the PGA. Augusta

National has negotiated to have only a handful of broadcast sponsors (five in 2016) that pay millions annually to share four minutes of advertising per hour of coverage, have very limited to no signage promoting their sponsorship, etc (6). More golf is shown per hour during Masters week on broadcast TV than any other tournament because of the exclusivity deal with the sponsors. Big dollars are exchanged for these exclusive broadcast rights and there's a whole vibe that this week is different than others on the PGA schedule. For a long time, the tournament organizers were only allowing broadcast coverage of the second half of the course.

Year after year, hundreds of players approach the first tee of all major golf tournaments with the same statistical chance to win. A guesstimate is that 20% of the players at each tournament are playing it for the first time. At Augusta, seasoned veterans who have played there before probably have their own experiences to draw upon. The other major American golf tournaments such as the U.S. Open and PGA Championship are held at sites that are selected years in advance. A limited number of venues exist that have the capacity to support large throngs of paying spectators and test the players accordingly. The top ranked players will often play at these tournament venues before the actual competition but that doesn't substitute for being a member and playing the same course day after day. Now that travel is so convenient, it's rare when a top-ranked player doesn't play in a major tournament. Injuries and family issues are the most common reasons why top-ranked players bow out.

Only a few players in recent history have had any local experience at Augusta National. It wouldn't hurt if you're a member, but chances of that are very slim. If you happen to be on the Georgia Regents University golf team, you get a chance to play once a year at Augusta National [4]. It's possible that some of the other teams have a connection to Augusta such as teams at Georgia Tech, the University of Georgia, or Emory. It doesn't hurt to volunteer at Augusta like local product and 1987 Masters Champ Larry Mize who operated the scoreboard as a teen, years before his win [5].

Augusta National is a technically challenging course but one of fixed constraints. Dog-leg left holes can't be instantly transformed into dog-leg rights. Bunkers are generally not going to be moved. Trees are planted, grow and die, and creeks and lakes are going to be in the same places year after year. The topology of the course doesn't change much either unless the earthmoving equipment is applied there. There's some sense that certain courses are better suited to one type of player over another. Longer hitters who are accurate are blessed with shorter approach shots, and players who can position themselves into more ideal locations on the golf course are at a distinct advantage. Some players like to play on Bermuda grass while others prefer other turf such as Rye or Poa annua. The presence of experienced caddies can act as a sort of equalizer in terms of overall course knowledge, but there's probably no substitute for on-site experience and prior success. With technological advancements in equipment, championship tee boxes have been moved back to lengthen the course and some grooming modifications can be performed, but Augusta National is about as close as one can come to the same challenge year after year.

DOES PRIOR SUCCESS AT THE MASTERS TOURNAMENT SUGGEST THAT THAT SAME MAGIC CAN BE REPEATED?

Magnolia Lane at The Masters at Augusta. *Credit: Shutterstock*

The answer is yes. Let's compare several different tournaments— The Masters to the PGA Championship, to other majors, and to two non-major tournaments that are commonly held at or near the same venue.

Going back to the inception of the Masters Tournament through 2018 (noting it wasn't held for four years during WWII) there have been 37 one-time winners and 44 years in which a repeat winner has won the tournament (including their first win). That includes Patrick Reed's win at the most recent Masters Tournament in 2018, the fourth consecutive year in which a new winner took the Masters title. Will he be a repeat winner or not at Augusta? History says there's *a* ~54% *chance* that a prior winner will win at Augusta again. That's highest among all majors.

The comparison of the number of repeat winners for several different tournaments, including the majors, is shown in Figure 1. What is it about multiple Masters winners like Tiger Woods, Jack Nicklaus, Gary Player, Arnold Palmer and Phil Mickelson that makes them different than Craig Stadler, Bob Goalby, Ian Woosnam, and Cary Middlecoff, who were one-time winners of the Masters? All were good enough to win once, but the combination of their games plus age plus other intangibles didn't lend itself to a repeat performance for the second group.

Back in the day, the odds were better. In the formative years of the Masters, there were 72 players for the inaugural Masters Tournament in 1934 [7]. Attendance varied, as low as 59 players in 1940 [8], and by 1960, there were 83 registrants and 45 players after the cut [9]. As time has progressed, the 2000 and 2010 Masters featured 95 and 96 players respectively [10,11]. So, if one has to play better than just a few play-ers, the odds are better. But as the field gets larger, there is less margin for error. That's true for the other Majors as well.

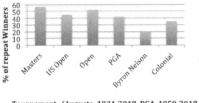

Tournament (Augusta 1934-2018, PGA, 1958-2018, all others 1945-2018)

HOW DOES THE MASTERS STACK UP AGAINST OTHER MAJORS?

The major with the second highest percentage of repeat winners is the Open (British) Championship, held each year in the United Kingdom. The Royal and Ancient Golf Club (The R&A), based out of St Andrews, Scotland, sanctions the Open Championship, which rotates between 10 different venues—five in Scotland, (the Old Course at St Andrews, Royal Troon, Turnberry, Carnoustie, and Muirfield), four in England (Royal courses at Lytham, Liverpool, Birkdale, and St Georges), and a course in Northern Ireland (Royal Portrush), that will only hold its second Open Championship in more than 60 years in 2019.

It's only been held at Liverpool twice, so the Open has functionally rotated between eight venues in the UK and nowhere else beyond these venues since 1931 even though the R&A claims that there are 10 in the rotation. While greater than the Masters' single location, eight is still a rather small list for tournament locations over the most recent 87 years. Perhaps not coincidentally, the % of repeat winners at the Open Championship is 52%, just behind the Masters.

Since the Open Championship started moving between venues, Harry Vardon, Tom Watson, and Peter Thompson have won the tournament the most times. Vardon won the Open six times at three different courses. Tom Watson is the modern equivalent of a links slayer, having won five different times, all at different venues (Troon, Muirfield, Carnoustie, Turnberry and Birkdale). To be able to win the Open Championship in five different places says something about one's ability to play links-style golf. Even more impressive is that on a return trip to Turnberry at age 59 in 2009, Watson came within a single stroke of walking away with a sixth Open Championship, having won at Turnberry 32 years earlier. Stewart Cink, who beat Watson in that Open Championship playoff in 2009, was three-years-old when Watson won at Turnberry for the first time. We doubt Cink was following Watson's moves at Turnberry during his first win.

The Masters at Augusta. *Credit: Shutterstock*

Of course, the U.S. Open and PGA Championship are both major tournaments that rotate to different courses across a much wider realm than the UK. Both of these tournaments recruit most of the top players in the world and allow more players to compete through qualification tournaments. In terms of repeat venues since 1925, the courses where the U.S. Open has been held most frequently include nine times at Oakmont Country Club (Pittsburgh Pennsylvania), five times at Merion Golf Club (Ardmore, Pennsylvania), five times each at Winged Foot and Shinnecock Hills (New York-based clubs), six times at Oakland Hills (Bloomfield Hills, Michigan), and seven times at Baltusrol Golf Club (Springfield Township, New Jersey). The scarcely repeating schedule and increasing movement to expand venues outside of the northeast have led to no repeat winners of US Opens at any single venue. Repeat winners at the US Open occur ~45% of the time.

No PGA Championship venue has hosted the event more than four times since its inception. There's some overlap with the US Open venues including Baltusrol (two PGA Championships), Oakmont (one PGA) and Oakland Hills (three PGAs), but no winners won the PGA and US Open at the same venue. Tiger Woods was lucky enough to find Medinah Country Club as the host of two different PGA Championships only seven years apart (1999 and 2006), winning both events. Medinah also sponsored three US Opens, but the last US Open at Medinah was hosted in 1990. The PGA repeat rate is even lower than the US Open at 42%.

OTHER LONG-STANDING TOURNAMENTS

The PGA Championship has been held in a tournament format relative to match play since 1958. With Brooks Koepka's win in 2018, there have been 36 one-time winners and 26 years where repeat winners were crowned (including the year of their first win). Thus, while the tournament moves around, there's no real advantage for prior winners playing head to head on a new course with its attributes and nuances. That translates into only a 42% chance that a winner is going to be coming from the pool of prior winners. Pretty high, but not as high as at Augusta.

Let's also compare two other tournaments that have been hosted for a long time. One tournament was originally known as the Byron Nelson Invitational and run out of the Dallas area. The other was the Colonial National Tournament—now called the Ft Worth International Open—historically sponsored by the Colonial Country Club in Ft Worth Texas. These tournaments were commonly run in May in subsequent weeks to reduce the travel issues for playing professionals.

The Nelson ran infrequently from 1944 to 1956 and annually since 1957 and has been played at multiple courses—although it's been a regular fixture at the Tournament Players Championship Course near DFW airport since about 1983, and moved to a new venue for 2018. Byron Nelson was a legend in the Dallas area and lent his credibility to the development of a local tournament. It also had decade-plus stints at Oak Cliff in southwest Dallas (1958-1967) and in north Dallas from 1968-1982. The TPC type courses are designed rather wide open as stadium golf courses, with identified locations for large bleachers to be situated during tourney weeks.

Alternatively, Colonial looks a lot like Augusta National, with one venue being used since the 1940s missing only two years in its history. The tournament has always been at Colonial Country Club and sponsored by the members for many years. Colonial Golf Club was the local course for Ben Hogan, another golf legend and nine-time major winner. Colonial is a shorter and tighter, leafy course, and players are punished for being errant in the tee shots in the woods between holes. It's not a surprise that players who might play well in an open format might be more challenged at a venue like Colonial. Perhaps more directly, it's possible that players opt to play in the one tournament that's more attuned to their playing style. Both the Byron Nelson and Colonial tourneys are named tournaments now with sponsors, but the general scheme of two tournaments in May of each year in the Dallas Ft. Worth metropolitan area remains.

The Dallas tournaments run across several venues and have produced 52 one-time winners and 13 repeat winners, corresponding to a 20% rate of multiple wins. Compare that to Colonial where in 72 total tournaments, 47 winners have been one-time winners while the other 25 titles have been won by players with more than one win in Ft Worth—a 35% multiple win rate. The rate of multiple winning is higher in Colonial compared to the Nelson, but both percentages are much lower than Augusta National (54%).

One rationale why repeat wins at Augusta and at the PGA are more common than in the Dallas/Ft Worth events is that the prestige and status of winning a Major tournament will draw the best players every year. It might be easier for one of the best players to win in a less competitive field at a non-major tournament because there may be potential winners who opt not to play every week to avoid injuries and the wear and tear of a long and busy pro season. As an example, Tiger Woods, who could have been very competitive in his prime at Colonial, chose to limit his schedule and commonly played the Nelson much more often than Colonial. In fact, the only year Woods won the Nelson (1997), he also played at Colonial the next week and finished fourth. In reality, players that could win a less prestigious tournament might opt out due to their own scheduling issues, overexertion, fatigue, burnout, and injury—particularly if the venue has proven to be a challenge in the past.

Another feature that might be tipping the scales in favor of the players who have already performed well is that tournament leaders have later tee times. Players at the Masters typically see most holes that have nearly the same pin placements year after year. The later groups can also watch highlights of the earlier groups, reinforcing where to be aggressive and when to hold back. One thing that cannot be accounted for is the weather, and it's possible for the weather to be worse or more accommodating as a given day progresses.

It's interesting to observe that at Augusta National, the deck seems stacked a little against players who have not won a Masters before and rookies who are experiencing the course for the first time and handling their nerves against a group of wily veterans and prior winners. It's a mystical place that explains a little bit about patrons (they don't call them fans there) and players are gobsmacked and overwhelmed. This deeper dive offers an idea about why there's so much emphasis placed on past majors winners, particularly at Augusta National.

EUGENE, OREGON: MODERN MECCA OF TRACK AND FIELD

Kenya's greatest export: Elite Kenyan runners including Dennis Kimetto, Eliud Kipchog and Wilson Kipsang run with Tilahun Regassa (3rd from left) at the front of the Virgin Money London Marathon on April 26, 2015, in Isle of Dogs, London, England, UK. *Credit: Shutterstock*

DOES WHERE YOU RUN MATTER?

I f the world's track and field athletes had their own hajj leading to a "track and field" Mecca—a running pilgrimage—where would that be? There are only a few venues in the world that are that steeped in tradition to warrant being on a runner's bucket list. Tops is probably the Panathenaic Stadium in Athens—a completely marbled venue, resurrected from ancient ruins that were originally built in the fourth century [1]. This stadium was home to the first modern Olympics in 1896, hosting four of the nine events, including all of the track and field events and the marathon. A close second on the list is Kamariny Stadium in Iten, Kenya—a far more modest venue than Athens, but it's human allure more than compensates for its lack of marble. Hundreds of runners from the Kalenjin Tribe and others work their way around the track at all hours [2].

Iten, Kenya, sits at 7800 feet of elevation. That's one reason why training there matters. The predominance of Kenyan and Ethiopian runners in middle to long distance races was immediately evident in the 1968 Olympics that were held in Mexico City at an altitude of over 7000 feet, more than twice the elevation of any modern summer Olympic competition ever held. The Africans training at elevation at home was a distinct advantage relative to other low landers who were still acclimating in advance of the competitions[14]. It had been well established by the Nobel scholar and physiologist A.V. Hill in 1925 that exertion at altitude resulted in an oxygen debt could result in lactic acid being produced in muscles during exertion. The lactic acid was then converted to glycogen during the recovery and rest periods[15]. The lack of oxygen when one exerted themselves at altitude resulted in longer recovery periods and diminished performance in subsequent exertions in the low landers. Over time, that acclimation results in humans at altitude increasing their hematocrit level to accommodate the oxygen debt. Those who are conditioned to training at altitude have already compensated for this transition and usually have higher blood oxygenation potential. And if one can be acclimated at high altitude with that high hematocrit and pop down for a race at low altitude, it's a lot less work to perfuse one's way through a race. But if you hang around on the beach acclimating at sea level, that raised hematocrit effect is lost over a period of weeks.

| *Credit: letsrun.com*

In the US, the two most noted track and field stadiums are in Pennsylvania and Oregon, at Franklin Field at the University of Pennsylvania (which hosts the Penn Relays), and at Tracktown USA. Tracktown is also known as Hayward Stadium—home of the University of Oregon track and field teams and there are some great stories and lore about that.

BEFORE NIKETOWN, THE PENN RELAYS

The Penn Relays are the oldest and largest track and field competition in the U.S., dating back to 1895. They have been held annually every April. Franklin Field has a rich history as a multisport facility, hosting high school events, the Penn Quakers NCAA football team, and the Philadelphia Eagles of the NFL, among others [3]. League requirements from the NFL about playing on a grass surface led to Eagles to a new stadium, but the Quakers still play at Franklin although, even though it's wildly oversized for the crowd the Quakers draw. The stadium seats roughly 53,000 spectators, while attendance at Quakers football games was less than 6,000 in the fall of 2017.

The Penn Relays occur over a three-day period and average ~35,000 fans per day [4]. Wikipedia has a list of dedicated track and field facilities with a capacity of more than 50,000 spectators, and Franklin Field is the only field in the U.S. on the list of 37 [5].

PHILADELPHIA, Pennsylvania: A pack of runners round the fourth turn in the Olympic Development mile run at the 2012 Penn Relays April 28, 2012 in Philadelphia. *Credit: Shutterstock*

EUGENE: NOT JUST HOME TO ANIMAL HOUSE! OR YOU MAKE ME WANT TO... RUN..... RUN...

Eugene sits on the Willamette River and is the hometown campus of the University of Oregon Ducks, who sport gaudy green and yellow team colors and one of the most irreverent mascots in sport. It's also home to a skunkworks that laid claim to the origins of the Nike Corporation, as well as hometown to middle-distance legend Steve Prefontaine. Eugene is an idyllic college town whose campus you might recognize. The University of Oregon allowed their school to be overtaken one summer in the 1970s to film the classic, Animal House—not knowing what hooligans to whom they gave the keys to the school.

Hayward Field, like Franklin Field, was a multipurpose track that hosted football games each fall. Named after Bill Hayward, legendary track and field coach at the University of Oregon, the field was built in 1919 [6]. Hayward was an athlete from Toronto who excelled in a variety of sports, including track and field. After he was done competing, he took over a rudderless Oregon track and field program in 1904 and coached them until the end of his life in 1947. Hayward was an influential member of the coaching community, linked with the fledgling Olympic games, and participated as an assistant Olympic coach from 1908 through 1932. Bill Hayward was such a legend that at the first game played at the new Hayward Field in 1919, he missed the dedication of the field in his honor because he was in the locker room at halftime, doubling as the trainer for the Oregon football team. Coaching salaries must not have been what they are now.

EUGENE, Oregon: JULY 4, 2016: Overall view of the stadium during day 4 of the USATF Olympic Trials for track and field at Historic Hayward Field in Eugene, Oregon. *Credit: Shutterstock*

Originally slated as a football stadium, a six-lane cinder track was added soon after construction. The track began as sawdust and was replaced by more durable turf over time. The amenities were improved and the scoreboard upgraded. Larger numbers of seats and more permanent seating was also added to accommodate capacity issues, but even in 1949, those latest renovations capped capacity at 22,500 [6]. Compared to Michigan Stadium, with a capacity of 72,000 fans when it was built in 1927, or the L.A. Coliseum that could seat over 100,000 fans, Hayward was an intimate setting, but large enough to host track and field competitions like the Penn Relays and NCAA championships.

As football's popularity expanded, so did the need for more seating. A few University of Oregon games were played in a larger stadium in Portland until inevitably, the University concluded that it needed to build a dedicated football stadium. The last football game ever played in Hayward was at the end of the 1966 season against the Washington State Cougars. One can find a link on the Washington State YouTube account where archivists painstaking digitized the black-and-white video footage from that last Oregon football game at Hayward where the Ducks lost to WSU, 14-13 [7]. With the construction of a new football stadium on campus, the athletic department allowed Hayward to be converted to a dedicated track and field stadium. Following the decision, Hayward hosted a number of high profile competitions, including the U.S. Olympic track and field trials in 1972, 1976, 1980, 2008, and 2012, as well as the NCAA Championships several times. With these important events came a new nickname for Hayward: Tracktown USA.

Following the death of Bill Hayward, Oregon track and field was able to draw on its steeped tradition and hire Bill Bowerman as its track and field coach. Bowerman had interests in sports distribution and technological advancements and ran a little side business called Blue Ribbon Sports that ultimately became Nike. Bowerman towered over the track and field community and had a laboratory at his disposal to test equipment and training schemes—the University of Oregon. He recruited excellent athletes, including Steve Prefontaine, a brash and opinionated Oregonian kid who Bowerman knew would turn into something. Something indeed.

Credit: Shutterstock

PRE

Steve Prefontaine (nicknamed Pre) was a competitive kid who played all kinds of sports before high school. He discovered early on that he was a reasonably fast runner and dedicated himself to developing into an elite high school distance runner at Marshfield High School in Coos Bay, Oregon, under coach Walter McClure, Jr. Prefontaine's enrollment at the University of Oregon may have already been preordained based on the fact that McClure had run under Bowerman at Oregon, and McClure's father had run for the legendary Bill Hayward before that. Prefontaine was highly recruited by national track and field powers, but a compelling letter from Bowerman helped convince Prefontaine to commit.

Under Bowerman's tutelage, Prefontaine worked to develop a running style counter to a lot of other runners. Many elite runners would conserve energy at the beginning of the race and kick for home at the conclusion. Prefontaine's opinion was that his competitors shouldn't have it so easy. If the others ran too easily, he would come out fast, trying to build an insurmountable lead by the end of the race when others increased their pace. The plan worked. Prefontaine was unstoppable at Oregon, undefeated in collegiate races longer than one mile.

He excelled at the long distances (between 5k and 10k) and developed legions of fans in track and field for being outspoken, brash, and larger than life.

Prefontaine's dominance rose to another level at Hayward Field. He set a American record in the 5k at the 1972 U.S. Olympic Track and Field Trials held at Hayward, although he was beaten in the Olympic games in Munich, finishing fourth [8].

Far too early, Pre died at age 25. He crashed his MGB convertible in the hills of Eugene after dropping off training partner Frank Shorter (marathon gold medalist at the Munich Games) the night after winning an NCAA 5k preparatory race against a group of elite Finnish runners. The location of the crash was less than a half-mile away from Hayward Field.

Nike, runners in Eugene, and Hayward Field are symbiotic. Nike is now a Beaverton, Oregon-based company and is the world's largest supplier and manufacturer of athletic apparel, valued at over $29 billion. Nike co-founder Phil Knight ran track and field at Oregon and co-developed the Nike concept with Bowerman. The two have been large philanthropic contributors to the University of Oregon and Hayward Field. A statue of Bowerman stands at Hayward Field commemorating Bowerman's contributions. Knight contributed more than $10 million to support recent renovations to Hayward, which are due to be completed in 2020. Let's hope that the special sauce that exists will survive the renovation.

Hayward has a mystique [10]. New Nike hires to the corporate offices visit Eugene and Hayward Field to get a sense of how special Eugene is to a company based 100 miles away. Eugene also draws sponsored runners to Nike for biometrics analysis, custom shoe construction, and other performance assessments and there just happen to be a plethora of chances to run together and in competition.

Hayward has been the backdrop for some phenomenal performances over the years. In addition to Prefontaine's U.S. 5k record in 1972, just a few years later in 1982, Hayward was the home for one of the most improbable records set in the most modest of circumstances [11]. Mary Decker Slaney, one of a number of elite athletes to call

Eugene home, was returning to Oregon to recover from the summer track season in Europe. On the flight, she ran into another Eugene alumnus, Roberto Salazar, who mentioned an all-comers event at Hayward that was scheduled the next day. Slaney had performed well during the European season and was near peak performance, having set several world records at shorter middle distances in the previous eight weeks. Slaney decided to registered for the all-comers 10k event the next evening. The extra rest refreshed Slaney and, while she would have needed to average 79-second laps to break the world record, Slaney consistently clocked in around 77 seconds that night in Eugene[11]. Slaney broke the world record by several seconds, mostly on a whim in her hometown, celebrated amongst friends and a supportive crowd.

TRACKTOWN USA PERFORMANCES VS. OLYMPIC PERFORMANCES

At the most recent USATF Olympic Trials, held in Eugene in 2016, American runners Justin Gatlin and Trayvon Brommell qualified for the Olympics with times of 9.80 and 9.84 seconds in the 100m dash. They later went up against Usain Bolt of Jamaica in the Olympics, where Bolt best them both with a time of 9.81 seconds—slower than Gatlin's time in Eugene. Brommell tailed off even more, finishing eighth in his final heat in 10.06 seconds and missing the final entirely.

It didn't get any better in the 200-meter race, LaShawn Merritt and Justin Gatlin qualified in Eugene in addition to Ameer Webb—all three sponsored by Nike—but only Merritt was able to make it to the final. Gatlin and Merritt were both credited with a time of 19.74 seconds in Eugene [12], which would have won in Rio de Janeiro if either had performed as well. Bolt took the 200-meter gold as well in 19.78 seconds. Webb and Gatlin failed to make it out of the semifinals as Gatlin has the ninth fastest time (20.13 seconds). Merritt, who also competed in the 200-meter, finished sixth in the finals with a time even slower than Gatlin's [13].

For a sprinter's race like the 100 or 200, there are many reasons why someone expected to do well might not win. They could be ill or have a sore muscle, a slow start, or an upset stomach. Maybe the weather wasn't great, and maybe everyone was too freaked out by Zika to perform up to expectations. On the other hand, maybe Eugene is the perfect place for track and field.

It's clear that Hayward Field has loomed over other awesome and record-breaking athletic performances. Perhaps it has an intrinsic special sauce that propels people to run faster. Perhaps a supportive crowd helps. Maybe the actual track surface allow runners to train more effectively. or is it the cool temperature or low humidity that enhance peak performance. Maybe it's the ghost of Steve Prefontaine. Maybe it's just a little bit about being at the right place at the right time, allowing one to push themselves just a little bit more.

What's striking is that little Eugene and its track seems to eke a little bit more out of everybody who runs there. Where the Big Sur Marathon is about the challenge of finishing and the Boston Marathon is about qualifying and participating, Eugene is about " just doing it" as the Nike slogan suggests. In Eugene, "it" is track and field. In the meantime, all four places remain on the bucket list of the authors. Wouldn't it be nice to log a few laps in a marble stadium or in Iten, Kenya just for fun?

THE WIDE WORLD OF CRICKET

Spin Bowlers, Doctored Surfaces, and the Case for Banning Zippers

The world of cricket is a sport and world unto itself. Cricket is similar to baseball, but much older, dating back to the 1500s and the British Empire. Both cricket and baseball are played with bats and balls. There are pitchers, fielders, batters, runs, dirt running paths, and grass fields. Pitchers (known as bowlers) throw the ball to a batter (called a batsman) who attempts to hit the ball and run, while fielders try to prevent runs and catch the ball. Despite these similarities, cricket and baseball are wildly different games and it's hard to resolve whether a baseball player would be good at cricket or vice versa.

Cricket game with a batsman and bowler in action.
Credit: Shutterstock

A BRIEF INTRODUCTION TO CRICKET AND A COMPARE/CONTRAST WITH BASEBALL

Key differences between baseball and cricket are shown in the table below. The rules governing cricket are called the Laws of Cricket and date back to the 1700s [1] and are updated several times each century.

	Baseball	Cricket
# of players on the field playing defense	9	11
# of batters batting simultaneously	1	2
Name of player who initiates play	Pitcher	Bowler
Batting locations	Near home plate	Near wickets
Foul lines	There is a 90° arc to the field that defines what is fair territory	Everything is fair territory (i.e. 360°)
Field dimensions	Roughly a diamond or parallelogram, 300-350 ft along the lengths and as far as 420 ft from plate to the fences	An oval ~450-500 feet
Match Length	Several hours. The match is based on 9 innings of play, unless curtailed by weather or extended by extra innings. Longer if pitchers and batters keep delaying.	Several hours to several days, and is quite variable depending on match attributes.
Pitch requirements	None specifically. Strikes have to cross plate in an identified strike zone based on the batter's dimensions. Wild pitches and pitchouts are legal.	None specifically. Ball must either bounce before encountering batter or be tossed at batter below waist height to be a legal toss.
Pitcher requirements	You have to pitch off the pitching rubber– there are no run-ups.	Must throw with a straight arm motion (but you can take a run-up)
Outs per inning	3	10
Bat	Tapered solid wood rod	Flat contact surface
Bat material	Ash/maple	Willow

| Comparing Cricket and Baseball.

The ball used for cricket consists of a cork core wrapped with string and finished off with a leather surface with slightly raised stitching around the hemisphere. The bowler stands—he has a run-up at an angle to one wicket, runs up, and pitches the ball to one of the two batters standing in front of the other wicket. The goal of the bowler is to get the batsman "out," by knocking over the wicket with the ball, (if the batter uses anything other than his bat to impede the progress of the which will hit the wicket then he is out "leg before wicket"), or to allow their defense to catch the ball if it caroms off the bat and into the field. All three instances lead to the batter being called out.

Balls that are hit and not caught are fielded, and while the ball is in play, batters run back and forth between wickets, which for the purpose of scoring runs can be thought of as two bases. If a batsman fails to reach the wicket before the a fielder hits the wicket with the ball, he is "run out," in a similar manner to a runner being tagged out in baseball. Running an even number of bases puts the same batter back up to face the bowler. Running an odd series of bases leads to the opposite batter batting. Each base counts as a run.

The key difference between baseball and cricket is that there is no strike-out rule in cricket—so that as long as a batsman can defend his wicket, and avoid being called out he can remain "in" and accumulate runs. One consequence is that a batsman tends to face the ball head-on rather than swinging from the side and is heavily padded (as in baseball, the fastest bowlers can deliver a ball at over 90 mph). Runs are cheap in cricket, and outs are extremely valuable (a player can have only one or two "at-bats" in a game).

There are today three main formats of play—the Test Match— played between national teams and lasting up five days (each day consists of three two-hour sessions), the "One day" game where each team is limited to 300 balls (pitches) each, which typically last for six hours, and the Twenty20 (T20) game, where each team is limited to 120 balls and is typically shorter than a game of baseball.

Strategy is adapted to the type of game being played. In the long-form versions batsmen are prized for their defensive skills, while in the short form offense is highly prized. In modern times the shorter versions of the game have become the most popular. In the long-form version, a batsman's innings (an "at-bat" in cricket is called an "innings") can last for many hours, and can accumulate more than 100 runs (a century). The longest individual inning recorded was by Hanif Mohammad of Pakistan in 1958, lasting 970 minutes and scoring 337 runs [2]. That's more than 16 hours of batting.

For someone who didn't grow up watching cricket, with the same batters potentially batting for long durations and running back and forth in the same path, the game can seem a little monotonous. Maybe this is why cricket is not as popular in America as it is in other parts of the world, though it was, in fact, the most popular sport in the US until the 1860s and widely played up to WWI. Generally speaking, bat and ball games are not very popular nowadays.

The game is popular in regions that were once part of the British Empire including India, Pakistan, Bangladesh, Sri Lanka, Australia, New Zealand, South Africa and much of the Caribbean. There's fierce competition and bragging rights that go along with winning a sanctioned match between these teams. The format for matches varies. A formal test match can be scheduled as long as five days, with both sides batting twice and the team with the most runs winning. Imagine being a spectator for one of these things. There are also friendlies that don't count officially and are demonstrations or trials simply to test things out. Friendlies turn out to be multiple days of practice to say, "You know, that was fun, let's do it again sometime." But they're still fiercely contested.

As in baseball, there are a lot of movements bowlers put on pitches, and angles and contact points with the bats vary greatly. Like any ball contacting a less-than-pristine surface, each encounter can result in unusual deflections that can carom off the surface and into the wicket scoring an out. The Laws of Cricket govern how a ball must be bowled. It almost always bounces on the pitch. So, the behavior of the ball is greatly influenced by the condition of the pitch. Thus, the process of trying to manipulate cricket pitches in the bowler's favor includes efforts to manipulate both the playing surface and the ball.

There are main types of bowling in cricket—fast bowling (anything between 75 and 100 mph) and spin bowling (typically between 55 and 65mph). Fast bowlers, as well as relying on speed, typically attempt to swing the ball in the air (away from or toward the batsman) and to make the ball carom off the pitch (which is typically made of very finely cut grass, whose roots serve to preserve the integrity of the surface). Swing is typically achieved by polishing the ball on one side while allowing the other side to become scuffed through wear and tear, which leads to differential resistance through the air. Unlike baseball, the ball is replaced only at fixed intervals according to specific rules, and in the long-form version the same ball can be used for upward of 500 balls (pitches). Slow bowlers rely on particular spins that they can impart to the ball, either through their grip or with their wrist as they deliver the ball. There are many different types of spin in cricket. A good batsman can predict what is coming since the ball is moving relatively slowly, so the art of a successful spinner involves deception—getting the batsman to misinterpret the type of delivery.

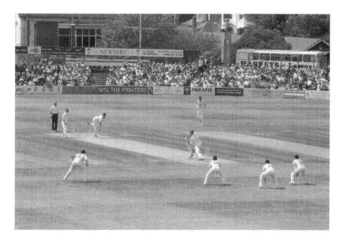

HOVE, England: The Australians take on Sussex County Cricket Club in the four-day Ashes tour warm-up match June 24, 2009, at the county ground. *Credit: Shutterstock*

TWEAKING THE CRICKET FIELD IN YOUR FAVOR

As in baseball, ball tampering is illegal. However, tampering is defined differently, since, as mentioned above, some treatment of the ball is permitted. This becomes important as the ball ages. Enhancing the shine on one side of the ball by rubbing against one's pants is legal, but using dirt to scuff the other side of the ball is illegal.

There's plenty of lore related to how host teams can tweak or prepare the field to accommodate their bowler's style. Since the game is played on five continents with widely different climatic conditions, the groundsman who prepares the wicket (also the name given to the strip of grass between the wickets) is usually under some pressure to produce a wicket that meets the needs to of the home team.

The wicket (pitch region) is 22 yards long and roughly three yards wide. Within this space is a protected area that is only two-feet wide and 56 feet long, centered between the wickets [3]. This is the bowling area. The players are prohibited from running in this area where the pitches carom off the ground as to prevent disrupting the field surface any further (because this might be an advantage for their bowlers when the present inning is ended). Efforts to run into this area are usually met with a warning. In some cases games can be played on matting— but they are not usually at professional level. I use my cricket machine on concrete—which is not dissimilar to the effect you would get on a grass wicket in Australia, but there's some expectation that in preparation of matches, the ground surfaces are likely to be excavated, watered, seeded, or otherwise prepped in advance of a competition.

In the U.K., it's commonly accepted that earlier in the season, so-called reverse swing pitchers tend to perform better in the wetter and lusher season. Swing pitchers tend to throw with pace and use the asymmetry of the seams or the smooth vs. rough side to coax the ball to carom either into or away from the batter. Hitting the pads of the batter is just as good as an out. The atmospherics in England makes cricket more conducive to swing bowling. If the batter is unable to put the bat on the ball in protecting themselves and the ball hits them, that's as good as the bowler hitting the wicket for an out. As the ground dries, spin pitchers tend to be more effective and throw a ball that excessively rotates by either a finger twist or wrist flip. Following the bounce, the ball rebounds curiously in odd directions. In Australia pitchers tend to throw a faster ball. In India, and other areas of East Asia, the lack of grass and more uneven ground surfaces create more spin pitchers.

Pitches are covered so they can't get wet (and you don't play in the rain). This wasn't always the case—and wet pitches favor a certain kind of spin bowler. There was one English spinner—Derek Underwood, who was generally good, but completely unplayable on a wicket on which it had just rained (which, of course, is often the case in England). He would not have been as successful if playing today.

Spinners can be effective in all conditions—it doesn't have to be dry. However, if a dry pitch starts to crumble, then they are devastating. India tends to have dry crumbly wickets, Australia tends to have hard bouncy wickets (so good for fast bowlers). But you get good spinners and fast bowlers everywhere—no country has a monopoly.

In 2012, it was documented that the Indian National Cricket Team captain asked a Mr. Mukherjee, the octogenarian groundskeeper in charge of the cricket field for the home team, to create a surface that would lead to more success for their spin bowlers in an upcoming test match with England. This kind of request probably happens all the time, but Mr. Mukherjee was outraged and called out the captain for being immoral. The Indian Cricket Control Board was obliged to provide additional staff to help prepare the surfaces accordingly. What the Indian team was surprised to find was that Mr. Mukherjee actually prepared the surfaces to neutralize the Indian spin pitchers [4].

This is a much-disputed issue. All groundsmen say they do not prepare wickets specifically for the home team. Most neutral observers would challenge this.

Of course, this isn't the first time a team has been surprised by the conditions of the playing surface. In the mid-1950s, England hosted Australia at Old Trafford. At the time, England had one of the better spin bowlers named Jim Laker. The Aussies were aghast at the decidedly dry and worn pitching surfaces. With ideal conditions, Jim Laker had little trouble dispensing the Aussies for one of England's best performances ever. Someone eventually talked and it came out that the groundskeeper at Old Trafford was advised by the captain not to water the pitching surface in advance of the matches [4].

| Cricket game action. *Credit: Shutterstock*

THE CRICKET BALL LASTS A LOT LONGER – A SINGLE TWEAK HAS A LASTING EFFECT

Looking beyond the playing surfaces, bowlers are relentless in their management of the leather on the ball surfaces. Pitchers, in particular, tend to rub the ball against their jerseys but only on one side, and use copious amounts of sweat and spit to lather up the ball on the other side. The goal is to keep one side wet and shiny and the other dry and rougher. These doctored balls tend to flutter as the wind takes the smooth side—a term referred to as reverse spin [5] which can wreak havoc on the rotation and trajectory of the ball [6].

This falls under the term ball management and each team usually appoints a player to be their dedicated ball manager [5]. Anything more elaborate to abrade the ball could be interpreted as going beyond management and veer into tampering.

In October 2013, a player named Francois "Faf" du Plessis, who was a bowler for South Africa in a match with Pakistan, was found to be polishing the ball numerous times against the zipper of his trousers [5]. This was deemed tampering and caused the umpires to dock du Plessis's pay, give the Pakistanis a five-run advantage, and change the ball [5].

More recently in 2018, the Australians and South Africans were involved in a test match held in Cape Town. During the third test, keen work by the broadcast TV camera crew identified Cameron Bancroft, an Australian pitcher, extracting a small yellow object from his pocket to rub onto the ball. Realizing he was caught on camera, Bancroft panicked and moved the contraband to his underwear after completing his doctoring [7]. Apparently this yellow item was a piece of sandpaper that he was rubbing on the ball. When questioned by the umpires, Bancroft suggested it was a cleaning cloth that would have been okay, but it was clear that this explanation was not truthful. Not unlike what happens when baseball pitchers are found with nail files and sandpaper in their mitts, Bancroft was ejected and has to sit out the rest of the test match[7]. Three team members in total were suspended for terms between nine months and a year [8]. The seedy feel of the scandal led to front-page news for a week in Australia and ultimately caused Magellan Financial to pull its $20M sponsorship agreement with the team [8].

If only the players were wearing sandpaper uniforms. Maybe that's next. The International Cricket Council apparently is aware of the lengths teams will go to doctor balls, and although they haven't implemented new restrictions, they were mulling over a ban of zippers on trousers as recently as 2015 [5].

It's wrong to assume all cricket balls are the same and the bowler is the only agent controlling the flight and movement of the ball. A recent study from the University of Adelaide investigated the physical and mechanical properties of five different commercial suppliers of cricket balls (who would have guessed there were so many?).

The results of the study found that only one supplier manufactured cricket balls to a consistent average mass [9]. The other supplier's balls tend to have a much larger statistical scatter and be either heavier or lighter than standards. With each ball expected to experience as much as five hours of play per match, it seems glaringly apparent that depending on who supplies balls and when a bowler is pitching, the consistency of outcomes through a match is highly variable.

Although the balls differ—it doesn't seem to be a big issue for the players. The type of wicket seems much more important. However, one interesting fact is that historically the ball is red, but once they started playing under lights they introduced a ball that was white, but seemingly manufactured in the same way. Yet white balls are thought to behave differently from red balls.

It's clear that cricket is similar to other ball and racket sports in that the field and the ball are oversized influences on both how they interact and how they impact the game. It's likely that weather and ground conditions result in game time decisions in cricket in much the same way they do in baseball. These factors can alter who pitches, how best to bat, how to defend the wickets, etc. The emphasis on how the field influences cricket is much more on the pitcher (bowler) as opposed to in baseball, where both the type of pitcher and the field conditions regulate how to play defense more than the pitches themselves.

Nonetheless, it's interesting to note that there's been just as much chatter about how to doctor the field and the ball in cricket as there's been in baseball. Small advantages can mean the difference between winning and losing and in the world of cricket. The impact of winning and losing is often calculated in terms of high salaries for top players and earnings for top teams. In this regard, cricket and baseball have found another common thread.

UPGRADING: DOES BUILDING A NEW ARENA IMPROVE A TEAM'S CHANCES OF WINNING?

New stadium construction in Minneapolis, Minnesota.
Credit: Shutterstock

I f you were to build a stadium for your team to play, and cost was no consideration, what factors matter most in helping give your team the winning edge? Domes are nice. They're climate controlled environments, but more expensive to build and operate. No air conditioning is needed in an open-air stadium, but open stadiums are also open to snow, rain, excessive sun, and other conditions that may be less desirable to fans attending the games. There's also the need to consider how to make up games that are rained out or canceled due to weather.

Some important questions that need to be answered include: How many fans should you accommodate? Where should your facility be located -near mass transit, near other facilities, near hotels? Who owns the stadium, how long is your lease and what are the terms of the deal? How well is the facility maintained and is it cost effective? All are imperative questions to address.

If you're already playing somewhere, you're weighing the liabilities and features of what you don't like about your current situation with the costs and benefits of trading it in for a different series of features. Separate the operational elements from the performance piece and for sports teams, it's just as relevant to consider whether the location and facility could enhance player recruiting and overall team performance.

THE LEGACY OF NOT GETTING IT RIGHT

BROOKLYN, NY USA - November. 27. 2012: Barclays Center is multi-purpose arena which opened in 2012, home of Brooklyn Nets Basketball team and future home to NY Islanders. *Credit: Shutterstock*

There are high stakes on getting arena plans right. The Barclays

Center in Brooklyn, New York opened in 2012 for the NBA Brooklyn Nets and in 2015 for the NHL New York Islanders. The move to support hockey games seems to have been a poor choice as the stadium was not designed for this purpose. Multiple outlets have reported obstructed views with the Business Insider calling some of the seats "the worst in American professional [4] sports." Some fans have sued for injuries sustained in the "cheap seats" over "defective design" where steep inclines have led to frequent falls and congested seats cause problems among the fans [5]. Furthermore, the Barclays stadium has been incapable of maintaining quality ice surface conditions suitable for a hockey game (see Chapter 3) based on structural design issues for the refrigeration system. The lousy playing surface has become such an issue that the NY Islanders are back at the drawing board building a new arena and have moved some of their home schedule back to their old venue, Nassau Coliseum[6] while a new arena is being built over the next three years.

The concept behind Little Caesars Arena (LCA) was build a downtown arena to continue the revitalization of the Woodward Avenue corridor in Detroit and to host the Detroit Pistons of the NBA and the NHL Detroit Red Wings. The Red Wings were already playing downtown at the Joe Louis Arena, while the Pistons were way out of town at the Palace at Auburn Hills. LCA opened in Detroit, Michigan, in 2017 and has been plagued by the dilemma of higher ticket costs and more prominent displays of empty seats. Maybe the Pistons are actually marketing themselves to a new clientele of fans given the large distance between the two venues. Maybe the marketing of both a new stadium and better group sales options are leading to a technical improvement in the balance sheet relating to ticket sales. But the scores of empty seats remain palpable on television. So serious is the empty seat issue at LCA that the Pistons contracted with a local furniture company (ArtVan) to produce black seat covers that mask the dearth of empty seats[7]. Putting more fans the seats is likely going to take efforts to both cultivate a new legion of local fans and to put a better product on the arena floor.

INSIDE VS OUTSIDE?

Since the Astrodome in Houston was built in 1964 and officially opened for business for the Astros in 1965, professional sporting leagues including baseball and football have housed home fields in domes, partial domes, and convertible domes. Without the ability to pass sunlight onto these fields, the surfaces played on in most of these stadiums are variations on AstroTurf: engineered polymer fabrics and carpet surfaces that are laid down and stitched together to look, feel, and seem like natural grass, but take more of the form of rubberized mats. The original Astrodome had grass on the field with glass panels installed on the roof to allow sunlight to do its work. But there were all sorts of issues, including instances where the heat and humidity inside the dome created pockets of high humidity that would actually rain inside the stadium.

The benefit to using domed stadiums is two-fold. First, fans can be uncomfortable sitting in very hot locales in the summer and cold venues in the winter. Domed stadiums allow for a more conditioned and controlled atmosphere. Second, for the team, uncertainties about weather can lead to rainouts and rescheduled games, which can create a series of logistical challenges. Getting through the season with every home game played as scheduled must be a large relief for team operations.

Currently, six Major League Baseball (MLB) teams play in domed stadiums—all of which now are retractable (listed in Table 1). Seattle and Minnesota played previously in non-retractable domed stadiums (the Kingdome in Seattle and the Metrodome in Minneapolis-St. Paul).

In the National Football League (NFL), there are currently 10 indoor stadiums, though some of the most famous have passed into lore.

City	Stadium	Retractable?	Year Built	Notes
Arizona	Chase Field	Y	1998	
Milwaukee	Miller Park	Y	2001	
Toronto	Rogers Center	Y	1989	
Seattle	Safeco Field	Y	1999	Replaced the Kingdome which was not baseball fan friendly
Houston	Minute Maid Park	Y	2000	Replaced the Astrodome that was built in 1965
Miami	Marlins Park	Y	2012	
Tampa	Tropicana Field	N	1990	
Minnesota	Metrodome	N	1982-2009	Built an outside facility

| Domed venues in MLB

City	Stadium	Retractable	Built	Notes
Dallas	AT&T Stadium	Y	2009	Replaced Texas Stadium which was supposed to be a dome but the builder left a hole since the 2 sides would not mate
Atlanta	Georgia Dome	N	1992	
New Orleans	Mercedes Benz Stadium	N	2017	Newest stadium in the league
Houston	NRG Stadium	Y	2002	
St Louis	Edward Jones Stadium		1995	Team left St Louis for LA in 2016. LA is building a new stadium which is also retractable
Detroit	Ford Field	N	2002	
Indianapolis	Lucas Oil Stadium	Y	2008	
Arizona	Univ of Phoenix Stadium	Y	2006	
Seattle	Kingdome	N	1976	Played until 1999
Minnesota	Metrodome	N	1982	Retired in 2013 after which the dome was demolished and replaced with a new fixed domed stadium called US Bank Field

| Domed NFL Football Stadiums

Terrible weather can invade northern cities (Minnesota, Detroit, Green Bay, Chicago, and Buffalo) producing snow, cold temperatures, and brutal wind-chill conditions. These conditions are amplified for players when warmer weather teams play northern teams during the fall and winter months. Warm climates (Arizona, Houston, Dallas, and Miami) can be excessively hot and can pose a constant heat-stroke challenge for the players and fans alike, especially when the preseason schedule starts in August.

MINNESOTA: WHERE COLD WAS A LEVERAGED ASSET

Only a few places have really embraced their local hardships as a home field advantage. Probably the best example is Minnesota and the NFL's Vikings. In the late 1960s and early 1970s, Vikings' head coach Bud Grant was known as an old school type of head coach who made the Vikings competitive before his retirement in 1985. The Vikings played outdoors in the frigid weather of Minneapolis, and as modern conveniences like radiant sideline heaters came of age, he supplied them for the visiting teams, but to maintain an edge with both players and fans, didn't provide them for his own team when playing in below zero temperatures. This created a need for all sorts of countermeasures, including old school tricks like Vaseline [1] on exposed skin, layers, heavy jackets, and the like.

Grant's decision to withhold heaters from his team was controversial and probably didn't make his players play any better, but perhaps it provided the Vikings a mental edge: looking across the field at the softies crowding in front of the heaters on the opposing sidelines. An example of this was an image from the last home game before the Vikings moved to the Metrodome in 1982 [2].

The fans ate up the "no heaters" policy and were equally overdressed and prepared to sit in the freezing stands for up to four hours at a time to watch the game. TV reporters and journalists loved playing up the heater issue every year. Granted, the thought of playing in Minnesota probably drove every Florida-raised player on the Vikings to blanch and look for another place to play—but again, this was another age.

Fast forward to the construction of the Hubert H. Humphrey Metrodome, that allowed the Vikings to play in a controlled, indoor atmosphere. A regular stadium with a huge, inflatable fabric roof on top, the inflate-a-dome strategy did a great job of keeping the field and stands isolated from the elements in January.

Once the dome was in place, the team had the same luxuries as opponents, but the ability to leverage the home environment was more of a challenge. One benefit was the loudness of playing at the Metrodome, which recorded some of the loudest decibel levels in the NFL—apparently a feature of the echo effect of the roars and chants reflecting off the fabric roof.

There was little difference in scoring totals for the Vikings or their opponents when comparing the last six years of playing outdoors (1976–1981) with the following six years of playing in the dome (1983–1988 since '82 was a partial strike year for the NFL). Statistics from Pro football reference.com shows that there was no dramatic statistical improvement in overall execution during normal downs, but there was a big difference in the kicking game [3]. The Vikings field goal kickers generally outperformed the visitors outdoors, and the average field goal made rate was ~7% better for Minnesota over the group of opposing kickers (62% vs. 55%).

Once the Vikings moved indoors, the made field goal percentage from 1983-88 went up to 71% for the Vikings and 79% for the opposing kickers. Extra points were equally dramatic. In the six-year outdoor period (1976–81), the Vikings' extra point percentage was 90% and went up to 96% after Minnesota started playing in the dome. The opponents had ~80% success outdoors, which rose to ~94% in the 1983-88 period. Minnesota essentially gave up their kicking advantage by moving inside.

In the end, a comparison of whether playing in the dome made the Vikings somehow less competitive is challenging. There's no question that the Vikings were an elite team before moving to the Metrodome. The Vikings won their division seven times in eight years as the Metrodome was being built. The Vikings were good enough to go to three Super Bowls in the 1970s, losing all three. Since the Metrodome was occupied, league expansion and a longer season have lowered the statistical probability of any one team going to the Super Bowl, much less winning it. It's now been over 35 years since those glory days, and the Vikings haven't been back to the big game since.

In comparing the performance of the other outdoor football stadiums in Buffalo, Chicago, Cleveland and Green Bay, of the four, Buffalo and Cleveland have been less than competitive, outside of the Jim Kelly glory years in Buffalo when the team went to multiple Super Bowls. Buffalo hasn't made the playoffs since 2001. Cleveland has suffered 19 losing seasons in a row, dating back to the end of the last millennium. Chicago won one title in the 1980s and has been to the playoffs four times since 2000, including one Super Bowl, which they lost in 2006.

In Green Bay, the team has overperformed, perhaps in part due to better management and an expectation in Wisconsin that they embrace the cold unlike Detroit and Minnesota. Lambeau Field is a lot like Wrigley Field in baseball—too steeped in lore to be torn down. There's some secret sauce between management and the venue as Green Bay went to the playoffs for eight straight years between 2008 and 2016, including their Super Bowl win in 2010.

Green Bay football fans walking to Lambeau Field in the cold

A broader sweep of the data analytics in football, comparing dome teams and outside teams during the period between 2000 and 2014, suggests that dome teams appear to field teams that also play worse in inclement weather. It is possible that the dome teams themselves were essentially not very good during this period, or maybe the rosters were tweaked to maximize performance at home in their dome. With the new capacity in data analytics, one will likely see more detailed assessments looking at more granular statistics that ultimately will be telling about any perceived advantage or disadvantage.

Overall, it's harder to think that the construction of a new stadium is some panacea to overcome poor draft selections, bad trades, bad coaching, and bad ownership. Stadiums have their own shelf life and the overall fan experience seems important enough that continuous upgrades and facelifts to the facilities need to be factored in, and in some instances new arenas are also needed. The Detroit Lions are a perfect example of a team that has exercised futility regardless of where they've played. It's possible that more quaint surroundings might lead to higher fan attendance, but ultimately, it seems that the quality of the product on the field is more important than where the team is playing.

THE LORE OF THE BRITISH OPEN

The scene looking over at the Old Course at St Andrews Golf course in Scotland, September 12, 2018. *Credit: Shutterstock*

The British Open, or the "Open Championship" as it is known in the U.K., has been played 147 times—the most recent tournament in 2018 at Carnoustie. The British Open is the oldest golf championship in the history of golf, starting in 1860 and tracing its roots to the founding of golf at the Old Course at St. Andrews in Scotland. The British Open is coordinated through the Royal and Ancient (R & A) Golf Club [4] and it's appropriately placed Museum at St Andrews in Scotland [5]. It has primarily been played at a handful of venues in England and Scotland, although the 2019 venue is scheduled for Portrush in Northern Ireland, a site that hasn't hosted the tournament in over 60 years [2].

THE EVOLUTION OF BRITISH OPEN VENUES

Since 1860, 14 courses have hosted the tournament, and of those, 10 are in the official rotation, albeit irregularly [2]. These tournament courses are all defined as "links" courses, or ones that have evolved into undulating ridges, carved by dunes, winds, and seas, into something approaching a golf course. The word "links" comes from the Scottish language and the Old English word "hlinc," meaning "rising ground, ridge" or hill [3]. The sandy soil in these areas made them unsuitable for farmland and didn't yield many trees, but the soil supported the growth of fescue (bunch forming grass) and bent grasses that allow the turf to harden. Links courses are typically hard and firm surfaces over which the ball can roll extensively.

The origins of golf are derived from the most natural of them all, St Andrews, where half the course (the outward half) is played going away from the clubhouse and hotel, and the other inward half is played in the opposite direction coming back. The undulations and other features of the course developed naturally—long before the development of diesel-based earth moving equipment.

Most Recent Tournament		First Tournament	Number of Times
2021	The Old Course at St Andrews	1873	29
2020	Royal St Georges	1894	14
2019	Portrush N.I.	1951	1
2018	Carnoustie	1931	8
2017	Royal Birkdale	1954	10
2016	Royal Troon	1923	9
2014	Royal Liverpool (Hoylake)	1897	12
2013	Muirfield	1892	16
2012	Royal Lythym and St Annes	1926	11
2009	Turnberry	1977	4

The tournament has evolved from a 36-hole, one-day venture when it first started, to the modern iteration with an extended number of holes, the evolution of the cut, and qualifying requirements. Functionally, other changes have been instituted, including how many players are playing together in a group, allowing the players who performed better to have later starting times, etc. [2].

For professional players who are used to extensively groomed fairways, rough that's cut regularly, trees for shade and windbreak, and conventional sand traps, links courses are pretty uncommon and potentially arduous playing experiences. While the greens are cut similarly to those of regular courses in the U.S., many areas of links courses are simply not cut but grazed by goats or sheep. Many possess reed grasses and rough in which balls can disappear. The lack of trees and the proximity to water usually translates to these courses being prone to significant winds and pretty crummy weather. Without wind, these courses are commonly defenseless to a strong ball-striker. Most of these courses have deep sandy pot bunkers that build up like dunes of their own. Some bunkers are so steep that there's only one way in and out, often on the low side of the bunker. If the low side is facing away from the hole, so be it.

The famous Swilcan bridge on the 18th hole of the Old Course links in St Andrews. The Clubhouse for the old course is on the left and the Hamilton Luxury Apartments is on the right. *Credit: Shutterstock*

VARIABLES: WEATHER AND WIND

One would think, okay, no trees, a few faulty lies, lots of undulating greens and fairways, let her rip. And some tournaments look like that. But sometimes the gods deliver weather challenges that shred large fractions of the field. A perfect example was the tournament held at Muirfield in 2002. After the first two days of play, the golfers nearest the cut played early and the better performing players received the luxury of playing late. What those players near the top of the leaderboard hadn't planned on was a storm that rolled in Saturday afternoon on the 3rd day of play. Justin Rose and Justin Leonard who were tied for 50th place at the beginning of the day played pretty well, each finishing four under par with 67. But they were done early. Who would have guessed that they would play themselves to the top of the leaderboard, finishing tied for third place at the end of an epic third round?

Steve Elkington, 1995 PGA winner, also had an early Saturday tee time. He finished early on day 2 Friday and was at The Auld House that afternoon—a local pub to Muirfield near a harbor where boats come in and out. Elkington tells a story of encountering the local harbor master who must have been straight out of central casting from the Pirates of the Caribbean movie [9]. The harbor master pulls him aside and tells him that "The weather is going to be s--- at about 3 p.m. tomorrow." [9]. Elk goes out, wraps up a three-under round and watches in fascination as he goes up the leaderboard hourly, from 40th, to 30th and also vaulting into the top 10 by the end of the day.

They all went up the leaderboard in part because the leading groups had to face a squall of biblical proportions coming off the North Sea at 2pm that battered anyone still on the golf course [10]. The harbor master was off by an hour. Players hit drivers into par threes, gale force winds, sheets of rain, etc. Most players playing at Muirfield that afternoon had among the worst performances of their professional careers.

While Rose, Leonard, and Elkington were relaxing having finished their 3rd rounds, Tiger Woods, then a young man with the first two majors of 2002 under his belt as wins and going for the calendar year Grand Slam, posted a dreadful 81, shooting himself out of the tournament. It took years for him to play poorly enough to exceed that, after encountering that fire hydrant in Florida in 2009 [10]. At least Woods had a reason to play poorly that day at Muirfield. Elsewhere, Colin Montgomerie, who had shot 64 on Friday at Muirfield posted an 84 on Saturday as well. Stewart Cink, who was often competitive in the Open Championship and won his only major at Turnberry in 2009, posted an 80. First-round leader David Toms who had won the 2001 PGA tournament and was in the hunt teed off into the muck and shot 81. Imagine seeing a crowd of players in the pro shop who hadn't tee off yet yanking every piece of rain gear off the rack, those who had already teed off were out of luck [10]. The great equalizer between the lower ranked players in the morning and the higher ranked players in the afternoon wiped out large fractions of the second round leaderboard. Ernie Els deserved hazard pay as he carded a +1 score for the third round in the height of the squall. He thrived when large fractions of the

Friday leaderboard wilted. The final round on Sunday was uneventful as far as the weather went, but led to a four-player playoff, with Els winning in the end. He deserved it.

Turnberry Golf course at sunset with the Turnberry Lighthouse in the distance. *Credit: Shutterstock*

THE BRITISH OPEN EVOLVES

The allure of playing these courses wasn't always what it is today, especially for players from the United States. In the 1920s, Walter Hagen and Bobby Jones each won the British Open several times (Jones also won as an amateur). Tommy Armour and Gene Sarazen both won at the turn of the 1930s. During WWII, no championship was fielded, and Sam Snead (1946) and Ben Hogan (1953) also won a title apiece. Intercontinental travel by air was rare and not easy and U.S.-based players had to come over and qualify before playing the actual tournament. For all of these inconveniences, the perceived value of the win wasn't worth the trouble.

As time went on, U.S. players continued to question the British

Open's qualifying rules. Arnold Palmer won back to back in 1961 and 1962 but actually competed in 1960 finishing a close second. His comments in 1960 were profound as he mentioned that the U.S. tour was rich in comparison and the need to qualify annually to play in the British was an impediment for other players who wanted to test themselves. The value for winning was not in the purse either as the winner took home ~$3500 in 1960 [1]. That same year, the Masters Tournament winner got $17,500 [7] and the U.S. Open winner got $14,400 [6]. Palmer also suggested organizing players based on their previous play, with those having played better competing amongst each other. Palmer suggested creating a scheme to pre-qualify tour professionals so that they didn't have to qualify each year. Palmer's interest was having won the Masters and the US Open in 1960, he felt that winning the British Open and PGA would qualify as a modern grand slam, replicating what Jones had similarly done decades before [1]. In 1960 Palmer finished second, one shot out. He came back and won the next two years of the tournament.

The difference between the Master's tournament and the British Open is that the Masters is one venue, while the Open Championship revolves around a grouping of similar courses. Win easily at Royal Birkdale, and that's great, but that course doesn't come back around to host its next Open Championship for a number of years. You don't get many second chances on the same course. That was less true years ago. For the first 13 years from 1860-1872, the championship was held at Prestwick club. In those 13 years, three guys, the Morrises (Tom, Sr. and Tom, Jr.). and Willie Park, Sr. won 12 of them. They each won four times and somehow allowed Andrew Strath to win in 1865 as the American Civil war was wrapping up. These guys mastered the Prestwick Course and had a better chance to win the Open Championship since it was held at the same venue (Prestwick) annually, just like coming back to Augusta National year after year and competing in the Masters.

Willie Park, Jr. kept it in the family, winning his second British Open back at Prestwick in 1889 after the tournament started cycling between three venues (St Andrews, Musselburgh, and Prestwick) after

1872. We dont know whether Dad was on the bag but it would have helped to have that local knowledge of the course. By 1890, the Royal courses at St Georges and Liverpool started hosting championships, and as time evolved, that's how the number of venues grew with nominally a 10-year cycle. As time has marched on, Prestwick and Musselburgh were retired and with it the dominance of the Parks and Morrises.

MULTIPLE WINNERS AT THE OPEN

Maybe it's worth considering how often multiple winners are actually winning on the same course. Of the multiple British Open winners in the modern era and ignoring the Morrises and the Parks (and two wins or fewer), Table 2 shows their names, and where they won.

Player	Number of Opens Won	Where
Harry Vardon	6	Muirfield, Prestwick (3), St Georges (2)
J. H. Taylor	5	St Georges, St Andrews (2), Cinque Ports, Liverpool
James Braid	5	Muirfield (2), St Andrews (2), Prestwick
Bobby Jones Jr.	3	St Andrews, Liverpool, Lythym
Walter Hagen	4	St Georges (2), Muirfield, Liverpool
Bobby Locke	3	St Georges, Troon, Lythym
Harry Cotton	3	Muirfield, St Georges, Carnoustie
Peter Thompson	4	Birkdale, St Andrews, Liverpool, Lythym
Jack Nicklaus	3	Muirfield, St Andrews (2)
Tom Watson	5	Troon, Turnberry, Carnoustie, Muirfield, Birkdale
Seve Ballesteros	3	Lythym (2) St Andrews
Nick Faldo	3	Muirfield(2), St Andrews
Tiger Woods	3	St Andrews (2), Liverpool

In terms of the theme that prior experience at one place increases one's chances of winning again later, what's impressive is that there are some players who play well in the links format, regardless of the venue. Hats off for both Peter Thompson and Tom Watson who seemingly could win anywhere. Watson, at age 59, held up playing against golf's best players through most of the 2009 tournament and finished tied for first place at Turnberry, a place he had known well and had won in 1977–32 years beforehand [11]. If he'd won at age 59, it would have surpassed the age of the oldest champion *of any major* by 11 years.

It's hard to imagine being able to outgun golfers in their athletic prime. It might happen, but it's more likely that a wily veteran out-guiles younger players based on prior knowledge or experience like Watson had at Turnberry. Unlike the other players there, Watson had decades of prior experience and had actually won at the venue before-hand even with a 10-year cycle for different Open venues. It didn't happen there that day, but if a senior golfer is going to win a major, it'll either be at Augusta or at the British Open, most likely.

There are epic stories to be told at these links [8]. They include the duel between Watson and Nicklaus at Turnberry in 1977, Jan Van De Velde's meltdown at Carnoustie in 1999 yanking out a driver on the 18th hole with a comfortable lead and finishing with a triple bogey seven to limp into a playoff ultimately won by Paul Lawrie. Tiger Woods lapping the field in a supreme effort at St Andrews, and Watson's near miss at Turnberry in 2009.

Palmer's pioneering efforts established the British Open as a normal challenge for U.S.-based touring professionals to test their skills. His winning also laid the foundation of how important this tournament was in the grand scheme of things and solidified The British Open's place among the great major championships in golf. Its storied history of 147 years is more than any of the other major tournament and its link to the grand links courses of the old world has made it something of a legend.

The rotating format of ~10 repeating venues suggests that playing well at one venue doesn't necessarily lead to much of an advantage in future years. The style and format of the courses are similar to the same type of shotmaking even if the courses look different. This is why a player like Tom Watson can play well seemingly anywhere on the isle and compete with the world's best at nearly 60. Good show!

THE AMERICA'S CUP

One expensive proposition...

SAN FRANCISCO, California: Emirates Team New Zealand and Oracle Team USA compete in the America's Cup sailing races in San Francisco, CA on September 12, 2013. *Credit: Shutterstock*

The America's Cup is a sailing competition far removed from a time when explorers lived or died based on their capacity to read the stars and interpret currents, wind patterns, and sail.

Technology has long since displaced the exploratory need of sailing but the raw cunning spirit remains today through competition.

There's a lot of history steeped in the culture of yachting. The America's Cup has been, at least in the United States, primarily the realm of land barons and the uber-rich going back to the gilded age. Yachting isn't a cheap sport. One who wants to compete in elite yachting needs to invest in computer-aided design, sea and air-based flow models, new keel, hull, and sail design—which aren't cheap. After that one needs to construct the yacht with advanced composites often produced by hand, plus the salary and training required for the crew to learn how to manage the craft in preparation and racing. These are full-time jobs.

There are a variety of different levels of yachting competitions. Among them include point-to-point races, like the Marblehead, Mass. to Halifax race that started in 1905, and the Chicago Lighthouse to Mackinac Island race that started in 1898. Around the world, there are races that take months to complete. Sanctioned races can also be guided by buoy markers, with the America's Cup being the oldest perpetual enterprise and award, started in 1851. Other races are much older. And rowing races predate yachting events by several centuries. There's also a type of racing that evolved called one design racing which was first promoted by an Irishman named Thomas Middleton in the late 1890s in which sailors sailed equivalently designed boats. The premise was that equivalent boat designs would identify winners based on skill and raw talent.

Competitions between sailors date back centuries to the Portuguese, Spanish, Italians, and Norwegians, all of whom had money and motives for exploration. The origin of a yachting competition between the Scots and some residents in New York started in 1851 [1]. The American yacht, named "America" sailed to the U.K. to engage in competitions with other yachts. One such competition pitted this boat against 15 other yachts around the Isle of Wight, located off the shore of Southern England [2].

America won that regatta and the New York Yacht Club received a trophy called the £100 Cup and later called the Auld Ewer or Auld

Mug for the win [2]. That same cup has since been awarded to every subsequent winner. For more than a century the American NY Yacht Club won every challenge of the Cup. These local races took place both off NYC and off Newport, Rhode Island, until the NY Yacht Club was finally deposed by the Australians in 1983.

That first series of races led to periodic challenges of the trophy, which started out infrequently (19 years between 1851 and the first defense in 1870), but challenges have surfaced every three or four years. Cumulatively, the New York Yacht Club remained undefeated for 132 years [2].

For the America's Cup, competitions evolved in which challenging boats hailing from different countries would face off to race the club defending the cup. There are competitions among different groups linked with the defending yacht club to ultimately represent the host country and the same type of competition happens among the challenging countries as well to lead to a one on one competition between defender and challenger. Eventually one challenger would be selected for each competition. The defending yacht club hosts the race and decides on the rules for the competition, dictating design, hull shape, geometry, etc., and both teams have to agree on the rules. If they can't agree, the race becomes a Deed of Gift match where there are set rules about boat dimensions described in the Deed of Gift and it is a similar one on one race for the cup which almost happened in 1988. Since then, the teams have tried to cooperative even if in a fierce competition. In 1983, when the Australian ship (Australia II) with a funky keel design that was a highly guarded secret, defeated the U.S. Liberty yacht [2], it finally broke the streak of 24 successful defenses of the cup by the New York Yacht Club. Since then, only the Italians, Aussies, and Swiss and the Americans have competed for the Cup as the ranked challenging team, although many other countries have sponsored challenging yachts that have not prevailed to the last stage. Among the U.S. teams, the Golden Gate Yacht Club and the San Diego Yacht Clubs have also joined the New York Yacht Club as defenders and challengers, again with other clubs that have sponsored boats that haven't made it to the final stage.

The American ship Columbia competes with the Shamrock in 1989. *Credit: JS Johnson photographer, from the Library of Congress, Prints and Photographs Division, Detroit Publishing Company Collection, Image # LC-DIG-det-4a21587* [4]

ANATOMY OF A YACHT

The components that make up the average America's Cup sailboat are complicated. Let's also review some important sailboat terminology. Everything above the waterline is considered the superstructure and the front of the boat usually comes to a point called the bow and the rear of the boat is the stern. The port and starboard sides of the boat are left side and right sides if pointed toward the bow. The mast is the central structure on which sails are fixed. There is a beam that is usually perpendicular to the mast and holds the main sail, called the boom. There's often a front sail near the bow called the jib that's also rigged to the mast.

Sails are typically made from engineered polymer fabrics, although other fabrics can be used. Often more than one sail is used and originally the goal was to catch as much wind as possible in a controlled way. Here things get somewhat technical, but most modern sails are really more like airfoils (think airplane wings oriented up and down. Functionally, the sail interacting with the wind creates a clockwise moment on the sail called the heeling moment and that can be enough to lift the boat out of the water. The motion of the crew creates a righting force moment and when balanced, the boat is stabilized or more level under the applied air force.

The goal is less about capturing the most wind but generating as much drive force as possible to lift the structure out of the water while minimizing drag and balancing the heeling force if it is too windy. Conventional sails of old were made from linen or cotton but have progressed to stronger and less hygroscopic materials such as nylon and polyester fabrics that won't get weighed down as much in choppy water and inclement weather. Advanced sails now have carbon fibers also laminated or otherwise fixtured to the sails to further increase stiffness. Sails are attached to masts that allow the sailors to adjust the tension and position of the sails. Underneath the boat is the substructure that includes the hull, and other fiducials including the keel, the dagger-board, rins, bulbs and centerboards, and the rudder, depending on the type of boat. The rudder pivots to steer the boat.

The goal of the hull is to not capsize the superstructure and to provide a low friction surface in the water. The keel is needed to provide ballast as the sails are taken by the wind. In the language of the boat builders, the keel is designed to provide a righting moment to counteract the heeling force component of the lift generated by the sails to keep the boat from slamming into the water. The longer the keel, the harder it is to cause wind to tilt the sailboat. Larger profile keels also have more drag in the water. In really windy conditions, the pull is so hard that one reduces sail area to reduce the chance of flipping over in the water. It's a fine line. There's also rigging, netting, cabins, steering mechanisms, seats, and brass hardware to fixture the jib sheet and sails.

Masts have historically been made from wood or metal and fashioned into poles or rods. These high load structures are now made from carbon fiber wound and oriented composites. There are fixtures called riggings to attach the mast to the hull or some other superstructure on the boat. The sail opening can impart a relatively large bending force on the mast and, in some instances, masts have broken under severe deflections due to high wind conditions.

Arguments abound in terms of which design is more competitive, one hull or two, but some America's Cup sailboats are catamarans or double-hulled boats made from carbon fiber reinforced composites. The goal is structural stability regardless of how many hulls. With many sailors moving from position to position, the hull shape needs to keep the boat from capsizing if the wind catches enough of the sail. With a strong enough wind, it's possible that one or both of the hulls of the catamaran can jump out of the water, supported by the hydrofoils. Earlier hull designs were made from wood, fiberglass, or other relatively strong yet light materials.

SEPARATING THE WINNERS AND LOSERS: THE DAGGERBOARD

The most secretive element of the AC-type boats and the one in which the view is most commonly obstructed is the daggerboard. Daggerboards are typically thin, strong, and often capable of retraction to give the sailors some control over the amount of drag the boat creates in the water. Some daggerboards even have the capacity to be rotated to alter the flow of water around it. Daggerboards are made from epoxy-based composite resins and integrated with the hull.

Daggerboards and rudders are thin foils because increasingly, boat designers have resolved that faster boats have less contact with the water. They have designed hulls and advanced hydrofoils to lift the bulk of the boats out of the water with only the daggerboard or foil dragging along [3]. The sails provide the force to increase the velocity of the boat. With enough air underneath critical elements of the boat, the boat resembles more of an airplane wing and in some instances comes out of the water leaving the hydrofoil as the only contact with the water with the ship flying along connected to it. The drag of a small foil in the water is much smaller than the boat itself and as the boat can drift airborne it might be better to consider the head of a yacht competing for the America's Cup as more of a pilot and less of a captain. Typical racing speeds are well in excess of 30 knots, and at higher wind speed, and with wind gusts, s boat speeds near 50 knots are achievable [3]. There is an upper limit close to 50 knots where the foils create a form of air bubble turbulence in the water and that increases the drag on the foil. This can now be done even in much slower wind conditions because of the modern sails that are increasingly efficient at translating the wind force into both a driving force on the boat and raising its ability to travel faster than the wind itself.

REGULATING THE COMPETITION FOR THE CUP

NEWPORT, Rhode Island: James Spittal skippers Oracle Racing during 2012 America's Cup World Series on June 28, 2012. *Credit: Shutterstock*

There are endless specifications for the America's Cup about boat, hull, and keel design to ensure some fair amount of competition. Those rules are published for each successive competition. The overriding rule of competition is the Deeds of Gifts charter that regulates who can officially compete for the Cup, which is rather open about competition. Yachting organizations from countries that bound open sea or an arm of a sea are eligible—including even landlocked Switzerland. The Deeds of Gift only describe that the tonnage of the competitors has to be between 30 and 300 tonnes. That's a rather wide swath.

As winners, the defenders got to define or refine specifications and put caps on the sail area and penalized waterline lengths on competing boats longer than 85 feet. In the 1890s, new yacht ratings were designated, including the requirements to shorten the waterline length to 70 feet. The biggest advocate for the new yacht ratings was a U.S. naval architect Nathanael Herreshoff who used advanced materials to create these long extensions off the bow and stern to leverage larger sail area. Every decade or two, there are new refinements which have led to class distinctions in yacht geometry including J class, M, class, and 12 meter class. The 12 meter boat designation lasted through most of the 1980s and was validated by boat dimensions that satisfied the following inequality.

$$\frac{L + 2d - F - \sqrt{S}}{2.37} \leq 12 \ meters$$

> Where L is the waterline length, d is the difference between the skin and chain girth—a technical detail about the curvature of the hull—F is the freeboard, which is a length from the waterline to the deck of the boat and S is the sail area in square meters.

Since 1988, there have been constant tweaks to the boat dimension designation including the International America's Cup Class (IACC) and now the AC designations, which spell out more explicitly general requirements for the boat dimensions. Interestingly, the America's Cup defense in 2021 is governed by a single hull requirement with a water line length no longer than 75 feet.

Big money is spent and proprietary secrets are held about design features of the boat, tacking strategies, and performance evaluations. Names of corporate titans who have waded into yachting include the Vanderbilts, the Liptons, The Turners as in Ted Turner, and Larry Ellison among others. The details about design features are guarded like national secrets, warranting top-secret classification. The defending champion's field advantage is stark, for they can choose how to configure the boat, as well as where and when to actually schedule the championship defense albeit with some tacit acceptance by the challenger. Maybe that's why the New York Yacht Club owned the cup for a century. Anyone who challenges and wins has to be overtly better than the former champion at sailing because every advantage is given to the champion before either ship sets sail.

In 1988, The San Diego Yacht Club with skipper Dennis Connor was selected as the challenging club to face the winning Australians in Perth. The Australians chose to use a conventional monohull boat KZ-1. The team from San Diego that was to challenge the Aussies interpreted the Deeds of Gift rules based on strict determinations that a catamaran with 2 hulls could be constructed to satisfy the design constraints. One proviso in the Deeds of Gift was that the boat could only have one mast but where it was situated could be anywhere. Even though both were governed by the same rules, the catamaran was so nimble that it won effortlessly four races to zero in a relatively unfair head to head with New Zealand's monohull boat.

Since then, catamarans have ruled and with each competition, general design specifications have been specific, regulating the general geometry of the boat, identifying other features of the mast, sail, keel and hull. The regulations while strict allow designers to optimize what they feel is important. In 2017, the challenger competition was completed and New Zealand, the challenging yacht went up against Team Oracle from the United States, and beat the U.S. team by a convincing 7-1 in races off the coast of Bermuda. As is the case for the winning team, the New Zealanders now have time to decide where, when, and how to defend their championship in 2021. New Zealanders will want to use this advantage in boat design and rules to give themselves a maximum chance to defend.

SAN FRANCISCO, California: Team Oracle USA racing in Louis Vuitton Cup part of the America's Cup world series on August 25, 2012 in San Francisco Bay. *Credit: Shutterstock*

CORKED BATS AND DOCTORED BALLS

From Pine Tar to Spit Balls

Major League Baseball has seen its fair share of attempts to modify equipment illegally. The majority of these schemes have focused on alterations to baseball bats and the ball. Throughout the history of Major League Baseball, attempts to alter equipment have been sophisticated and the players behind them stealthy in their use.

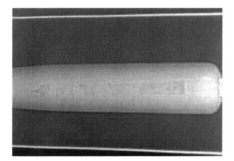

X-ray image of Pete Rose's bat which shows an interior core element of some different composition and density and what appears to be a taper suggesting the use of a coring drill bit closest to the handle. *Credit: Barry Petechesky, Deadspin.com*

BASEBALL BATS

MLB rule 1.10 states that the baseball bat should be a smooth round stick made from a single piece of wood (metal bats aren't allowed in Major League Baseball), no longer than 42 inches and no more than 2.61 inches at its widest part [1]. It is legal to carve out a section of the bat at the farthest end, called a "cup", but it can only be one inch in diameter. Rules also determine that the handle of the bat can only extend as far as 18 inches and can be wrapped, or covered, in an effort to improve the grip for the batter. No colored bat can be used, unless approved by the rules committee, like pink bats used in May to raise awareness for the fight against breast cancer.

Most bats are made from ash and maple—typically bleached woods —but, other materials have included hickory, birch, and bamboo. Densities determine the weight and strength of the bat and common MLB bat materials are shown in Table 1.

Wood is dried to harden the material and make it more workable. This process reduces the bat density and can make the bat easier to shatter on contact. There's a growing tendency for bats to shatter during play (primarily ones made of maple). This could be from larger contact forces from harder throwing pitchers, inferior quality wood, over-dried material, or players using bats so small in diameter that they fail under the bending load imparted when the ball contacts the bat. However it occurs, bat fractures are noticeable events.

Material	Density $(H_2O = 1000 \text{ kg/m}^3)$	Comments
White ash	650-850	Hygroscopic
Bamboo	300-400	Rare
Birch	670	needs to be broken in to harden surfaces
Hickory	830	
Maple	600-750	Hygroscopic
Cork	240	

Density of different woods commonly used for baseball bats. [2]

The typical bat used in MLB is between 34 and 36 inches long and weighs between 32 and 39 ounces (0.9-1.1 kg). Bat dimensions vary by player preference. For example, Vladimir Guerrero, a great hitter for the Expos and Angels in the late 1990s/early 2000s, used bats of different masses but they all had the same length [3].

While players have been particular about the bats they use, there have been players those who've attempted to gain an advantage by hollowing out the core of the bat and filling it with a different material [4]. These players have been famously caught when a hollowed bat breaks and spills its contents onto the field. The term "corked bat" is used for all types of bats altered in this way but is derived from instances when the filler material is cork. Why "cork" a wooden bat? What advantage does it provide?

CORKED BATS

From a physics perspective, there are several potential advantages to using a corked wooden bat. A corked bat has a lighter head, potentially increasing bat speed, while retaining length, to cover the entire strike zone. Another advantage is that impact mechanics of a baseball hitting a hollowed out cylinder, or one filled with foreign materials, will be different than contacting a solid cylinder.

Consider Vladimir Guerrero's 35-ounce bat. A one-inch hole drilled 10 inches deep into the end of the bat could reduce the volume of the bat considerably. Using a maple bat as an example (density of 700 kg/m^3), the volume is calculated using $V = \pi r^2 L$ (where r is the radius of the hole and L is the length of the borehole). The volume bored out is 3.14*(0.5 in*2.54 cm/in)^2 *10 inches*2.54 cm/inch=128 cm^3.

The mass of the bored section is 128 cm^3*0.7 g/cm^3 = 90 g = ~3.17 ounces. Thus, Guerrero's 35-ounce hollowed-out bat has the same dimensions as the original but is more than 3 ounces (~9%) lighter.

If the hollow bat is filled with cork or a foreign material and then filled with a small amount of wood filler to hide the bored out region, there is some additional mass added. Cork has a density of ~240 kg/m^3 so adding the same volume back in cork adds an additional ounce to the mass of the bored out bat.

What looks identical to a 35-ounce solid bat actually weighs only 33 ounces [5]. Why not just use a lighter bat? Lighter bats are shorter, so the player loses range over the strike zone. Using a corked bat gives a distinct advantage in bat speed and player reflexes.

Former MLB all-star Pete Rose played for Cincinnati and Philadelphia. Rose was a guy who scrunched up in the batter's box to make his strike zone marginally smaller and sprinted to first base after being walked in the hope of stretching the walk into two bases. There's ample evidence to suggest that Rose was also a serial corker.

Deadspin details a bat Rose used, and subsequently gave away, while he was chasing Ty Cobb's hit record. This bat was an authentic Rose, down to the scuff marks on the bat handle and his trademark #14 on the bottom [6]. X-ray imaging showed compositional differences in a center portion of the bat down to the tell-tale markings of a coring drill bit of acute angle nearest the bat handle. This led to the bat being cored out from the fat end. The bat wasn't hollow but had a filler material of subtly different composition. Rose was a contact hitter and likely never really tried to hit the ball hard enough to fracture a lot of bats. His role as a leadoff hitter was to make contact and get on base. Pete Rose has a tarnished reputation in MLB for a lot of reasons—corking his bats added to the list.

Other hitters of note were caught for corking their bats, like Sammy Sosa, Albert Belle, Craig Nettles, and Billy Hatcher [7]. Sosa was the latest on this list to be caught (2003). One reason corked bats may be on the wane could be the inferior quality of the wood being used for bats. Maybe it's harder to actually do an effective corking job without fatally ruining a bat these days. Once caught, players resort to any excuse to avoid blame. Most players claim to have no idea that a bat is corked. They might shout that they grabbed the corked bat by a mistake, that it was designed for practice, or that it was gifted to them in some way.

The physics of a ball interacting with a corked bat has been extensively studied. The general takeaways are that the exit velocity (the batted ball speed) of a ball encountering a corked bat is generally less than or equal to a solid bat. As a result, baseballs hit with a corked bat won't go any farther than with a solid bat. This is a disadvantage of using a corked bat.

The main benefit of a corked bat is that a batter can swing faster. This means the batter can wait incrementally longer before committing to swinging, and with this increased time the player can discern ball trajectory and rotation and can better predict whether a pitched ball will remain in and around the strike zone. This increased lag time should make the hitter more selective and result in a better batting average, fewer strikeouts and potentially more walks, resulting in the player getting on base more often.

MLB players play with corked bats at their own risk. If caught using a corked bat (if fractures while in play, perhaps), the batter is immediately "out", ejected from the game, and subjected to potential future league punishment including suspension. There's also an embarrassment factor and the stain that goes with using a corked bat. While the perceived loss in prestige may pale in comparison with failing a drug test, it's no less deflating to a player's reputation.

BASEBALLS AND ATMOSPHERE

Everyone seems to understand that baseballs hit in Colorado at a mile high altitude travel farther than those hit at sea level. That fact stems from the relative humidity and the lower number of gas and water molecules in the atmosphere (higher altitude = lower density = lower number of molecules). To illustrate the relationship, the viscosity and density of air are shown as functions of altitude in the following figures.

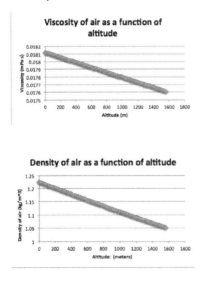

If all games were played at the same altitude, there would be little difference in how far a ball traveled. But this isn't the case. When a ball is hit in a gaseous environment as opposed to a vacuum, those gas molecules carom off the ball as they encounter the ball, slowing the ball down.

To understand the physics of ball motion one needs to recognize that gas has a viscosity. As the ball travels through a viscous medium like air, there's a drag force as the ball has to displace the air molecules and humidity contained in the gas phase to propel itself incrementally forward. A separate gravitational force is slowing the upward trajectory of the ball and forcing it back to the ground. That drag force is always operating, so the ball off the bat has a slightly larger velocity than it does when it bounces onto the ground. The viscosity of the air, while small, contributes to reducing how far the ball travels.

Coors Field in Colorado is at a high enough altitude (5,200 feet of elevation or 1600 meters) that it affects the ball trajectory. Every other field in MLB is below 1,100 feet of elevation (~350 meters). The difference in hitting a ball in Denver vs one near sea level is linked with a 3% reduction in the viscosity of the air through which the ball flies. Experts suggest the reduced air viscosity translates to a 10-15 ft extension in the length of a ball hit 350+ feet hit in Denver.

A second influence on how far a ball travels is the relative humidity in the air. The higher the humidity, the higher the viscosity as well, meaning balls that don't travel as far as they would in places where humidity is low. Playing in a rainstorm probably also reduces how far the ball can travel.

The Colorado Rockies use humidors to combat the effect of drier balls and thinner air in their home ballpark, Coors Field. In 2018, humidors are also being used in Arizona, the second highest MLB park at 1075 ft of elevation. The low humidity at Coors causes water molecules to desorb from the ball and into the arid atmosphere, drying them out. Humidifying the baseballs has an influence on the mass of the ball and reduces its viscous drag. Since using humidors, there has been an observed drop off in the number of home runs hit at Coors Field in Denver [12]. This success has led to humidor use at the Diamondbacks' home park in Arizona as well, which also struggles with low humidity at their ballpark and fewer home runs there as well[11].

SPITBALLS AND OTHER ILLEGAL MODIFICATIONS

Major League Baseball takes great strides to make sure that all balls used in games are the same. Alterations are often made by pitchers looking to gain an unfair advantage. A lot of pitchers take it upon themselves to doctor baseballs while on the mound. Tools of the trade include nail files, sandpaper, the dirt around the mound, sharpened belt buckles—almost anything that affects the surface and texture of the ball. Alterations made to improve the pitcher's grip on the ball or efforts taken to alter the surface to affect the ball's trajectory are called "scuffing" [8].

Alterations including the application of saliva, petroleum jelly, or other foreign substances are referred to as a "spitballs". The hardest thing about altering a baseball during a game is that the pitcher needs to do so while standing on the mound—in plain sight of fans, opponents, and the umpiring crew. With so many baseballs used during a game, altering one ball only works until that ball is hit out of play or otherwise removed. Once that ball is gone, the doctoring process must start over again. This rapid changing of the ball is unique to baseball and is quite a bit different than in cricket where a single ball is used for hours of play and scuffing it has a more lasting influence.

Credit: Shutterstock

Serial suspects of doctoring the baseball include Joe Niekro and Gaylord Perry, who unlike their corking counterparts, have garnered fame the way they were caught. Niekro brought a belt sander with him to the David Letterman show and Perry typed on a keyboard and otherwise paraded through the ESPN studios in a humorous commercial [9] touting their baseball-doctoring prowess.

Many players have been accused and searched, but overall, players are rarely caught red-handed. Kenny Rogers, who pitched with the Detroit Tigers in their playoff run to the 2006 World Series, was filmed with a peculiar dark smudge on his palm during Game two of that World Series. While Rogers was never formally found guilty, there was mass suspicion. The opposing manager, Tony La Russa of the St. Louis Cardinals, never asked the umpires to investigate Rogers because he "believe(d) in the purity of the competition." [13]Karma prevailed as the Cardinals won the series four games to one (the lone Tigers' victory belonged to Rogers).

The spitball was made illegal following the 1920 MLB season. At the time of the ban, those who routinely pitched with spitballs were grandfathered into its use, the last of which was Jack Quinn who retired in 1933. Adding a foreign substance to the ball alters the wind resistance and weight to one side as it flies through the air, changing its flight and causing it to move atypically. It may also allow the ball to slip out of the pitcher's hand without spin, like that of a knuckleball, but with maintained velocity. This makes the spitball potentially dangerous.

An MLB batter was killed when he was struck in the temple by a spitball in a dimly lit game in August of 1920, helping precipitate its ban. As spitballs were popularized, pitchers often used a mixture of dirt, spit, and tobacco on the ball, which stained it a dark brown color, close to that of the infield, making it difficult for hitters to identify.

Scuffing too can cause the baseball to float and flutter along with other strange rotations as it heads to home plate. Other efforts to alter the baseball include rosin, talc, pine tar, shaving cream, and sunscreen. Most of these methods, like scuffing, are designed to increase a pitcher's grip on the baseball [10].

The game is not always played under ideal conditions, and rain and cold temperatures can affect how well a player can grip the ball. There's lore on what weather and alteration combinations work. The goal of the modifier is to be discreet, as to not get caught—the fine line of being able to influence one's grip without coming out covered in rosin. There are plenty of places where pitchers conceal illegal materials, including in and around the cap, back of the neck, outside of the palm, on/in the glove. Anywhere a small sleight of hand can yield an advantage. Some doctoring is expected and tolerated, while obvious attempts to alter the baseball usually results in ejection.

It's funny to observe how far pitchers and hitters go to improve their chances against opposing teams. One can alter the bats and one can affect both the tackiness and texture of the ball, and the most prudent scheme for executing this is to do this rather clandestinely. The same kinds of shenanigans likely occur with other pitching sports such as cricket and one wonders whether such elaborate deceptions occur in other sports to the same degree.

Credit: Shutterstock

DEFLATEGATE AND INFLATION PRESSURE IN SPORT

Less Is More Unless It's Illegal

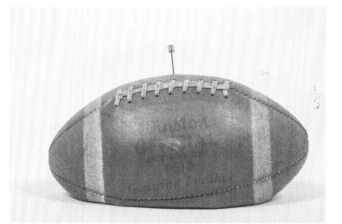

J anuary 15, 2015—the AFC Championship Game between the New England Patriots and the visiting Indianapolis Colts. New England easily won the game 45-7 in what became known as "Deflategate."

During the game, an intercepted ball was thought to be of lower pressure than league rules allow (12.5-13.5 psi or 86-93 kPa). By league rules, each team maintains the regulation balls used by their respective offenses. The Colts alerted the officials who checked the footballs at halftime and upon measuring found several balls for New England were underinflated. After re-inflation, the game played on but the aftermath of the possible deflation and the accusations of cheating for the Patriots and specifically their quarterback Tom Brady raged on.

An offseason NFL investigation ensued through tremendous press coverage. The NFL hired an attorney named Ted Wells who ultimately concluded there was no physical explanation for the lower inflation of the Patriots' footballs during the game, detailed in what was called the Wells Report. This led to a suspension for quarterback Tom Brady for his involvement, a $1 million fine for the Patriots, and the forfeit of their 2016 first-round and 2017 fourth-round draft picks. These were hefty fines and additional bad press (don't forget about the 2007 Spygate) for the Super Bowl champs. In fact, the Patriots seem to be without peer in terms of the level of documented efforts to gain an advantage, including stolen play sheets and playbooks, collected by lowly staffers engaging with the opponent [6] and stolen signals [7]. But the questions at hand include whether deflated balls carry advantages in football and does tampering with ball pressure happen in other sports with inflated balls?

DEFLATEGATE: BASKETBALL

The 1973 New York Knickerbockers weren't a particularly tall team and relied heavily on their shooters. This Knicks were a dominant team that included Dave DeBusschere (6'6"), Earl "The Pearl" Monroe (6'3"), Jerry Lucas (6'8"), Bill Bradley (6'5"), Walt 'Clyde' Frazier (6'4"), Willis Reed (6'9"), and future coaching legend Phil Jackson (6'8"). In a Chicago Tribune article by Sam Smith in 1986 quoted Phil Jackson as stating "The Knicks championship team of 1973 would literally take the air out of the balls and 'deaden' them as a tactic to offset a lack of height in the team's frontcourt." There were deflating basketballs, just like the Patriots championship team deflating footballs, only 42 years earlier.

Jackson explains, "What we used to do was deflate the ball. We were a short team with our big guys like Willis, our center, only about

PHIL JACKSON   FORWARD

6'8" and Lucas also 6'8". So what we had to rely on was boxing out and hoping the rebound didn't go long. To help ensure that, we'd try to take some air out of the ball. We'd all carry pins and take the air out to deaden the ball."

The NBA rule in 1973 recommended a fill pressure of 7-9 psi of pressure, and now the standard is 7.5 to 8.5 psi. Jackson mentioned that the Knicks wanted balls that were 7 psi, in their words, softer, but not necessarily illegal[1, 2]. Bill Bradley mentioned that they regularly deflated balls but only when he felt that they were above specifications or overinflated[3]. Of course, there was no gauge nearby to ultimately resolve that.

THE ADVANTAGE OF DEFLATING BASKETBALLS AND FOOTBALLS

Basketball and football are distinctly different sports. The scoring systems, player body types, and skills necessary to be successful can be unique. Two different sports, two different championship teams, both using deflation to gain an advantage. What advantage does deflating provide?

Phil Jackson mentions deflating providing less rebound with missed shots as the advantage for his height disadvantaged team. Let's look at the bounce response on an asphalt surface and compare its rebound off the ground from a level of 36 inches as a function of the ball's internal pressure. We actually measured this on Brian's asphalt driveway. The figure of merit relating to bounce recovery is called the coefficient of rebound restitution, e. This coefficient is essentially equal to the square root of the ratio of the rebound height and relative to the height from which the ball was dropped, shown below:

$$e = \sqrt{\dfrac{h}{H}}$$

Where: e is the coefficient of rebound restitution, h is the rebound height, and H is the original dropped height.

For a leather basketball, the variation in e with P is shown in the figure below. These results demonstrate a clear correlation between basketball pressure and rebound coefficient, meaning the higher the pressure the bigger the rebound. Ball construction, ball texture, and floor/rim/backboard characteristics all impact the rebound dynamics, but this illustrates the point: there is an almost 10% difference in the rebound of the ball and with proper positioning could result in a 10% increase in retention of possession going from 9 psi to 7 psi of pressure in a basketball.

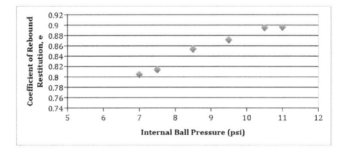

Aside from rebounding, the advantage of deflating a football could be advantageous in basketball as well: these balls may be easier to grip, handle, catch and throw. Football is often played in outdoor conditions making a deflated ball even more advantageous in wet or cold conditions where grip is made difficult. Additionally, as opposed to basketball where both teams will use the same ball in the back and forth actions of the game, a recent rule change in football led to team supplied specific balls that each team used allowing the advantage to be one-sided.

Control of the ball is a big advantage in both football and basketball. In basketball, players with bigger hands often have better basketball skills. The ability to palm the ball, for example, is a skill helpful for players to elevate to dunk it, do one-handed passes, and make it difficult for opponents to steal. Since the 1973 season, NBA players have been known to tweak the air pressure in the ball to allow them more control. The dominant center Shaquille O'Neal was also known to have a deflator nearby if he thought it was overinflated [4]. Shaq wasn't aware of whether he was actually reducing the pressure to below specifications, but he would take it upon himself to tweak the ball if felt it was too inflated, and he believed he was doing this in the best interests of all of the players.

It isn't just the ball pressure that makes a difference—brand matters, also. The ball type is another potential home team advantage in some sports. NCAA basketball has no official brand of basketball and schools will typically use balls from brands in which they have individual contracts while playing at home, be that Spalding, Wilson, Nike, or adidas [5]. Thus, a competition between two Under Armour schools, for example, may be more competitive as both teams will be comfortable with the feel and texture of those balls. In 2012, Mark Viera mentions that there were seven different brands being used among the 74 NCAA basketball teams in the big six conferences. The largest brand used was Nike, counting for 47 teams. Wilson was second with 12 teams [5]. This isn't a factor at the professional level as the league contracts with a single equipment manufacturer, thus everyone plays with the same brand of game balls.

Whether bending or breaking the rules, regulating inflation pressure can lead to an advantage in competitive sports. Were the 1973 Knicks and the 2015 Patriots correct in using this technique? We guess the proof is in the pudding. They're both champions.

IRVINE, California: An underinflated Wilson NFL
Official Football, like the one used in the controversy
called "deflate-gate". *Credit: Shutterstock*

JAI ALAI

More Than a Crossword Clue

Jai alai played today in the United States, is one of 20-plus variants of games deriving from those developed centuries ago in the French Basque towns of Spain's Saint Pée-sur-Nivelle and San Sebastian in the Pyrenees Mountains [1]. At least in the US, jai alai is an obscure sport not unlike the region from which it evolved. In the United States, more people know the name because of its use in the New York Times crossword puzzle seemingly every third Sunday. The name jai alai translates to "merry festival" in the Basque language of Euskera, and its name is attributed to the Basque writer Serafín Baroja who coined it in 1875 [2].

Baroja dubbed the game jai alai in part because of the party around the game. Jai alai was originally played as a spectator sport in the large cities in Spain inside grand industrial plazas seating as many as 2,000 people [3]. Among the crowd, there was a lot of betting, as in horse and greyhound racing. The sport grew due to a large number of Basque ex-pats who emigrated to Argentina and other areas of Latin America [3]. Jai alai had its heyday in the 1950s, gaining a foothold in Florida and from there to the northeast when parimutuel betting was approved in Connecticut [9]. When Cuba banned gambling under Fidel Castro, a lot of Cuban expats and players moved to Florida and patronized the jai alai arenas, called frontons.

Interest in the sport has essentially dried up in the United States since then, due to contractual issues between players and owners who didn't want to deal with an organized union of players, along with the rising popularity of lotteries, wider access to casinos and slots, and off-track betting. The players have legitimate concerns about player longevity with balls hurled with such momentum as to cause real damage. There is also this issue of essentially betting on people as opposed to horses. Now only a few frontons remain. Two full-time frontons still run in Florida today—one in Miami and one on Dania Beach [3]. Several others have a short season. Jai alai was sporadically played in the northeast through the late 1980s, but the sport is mostly extinct. Jai alai is non-existent in the western U.S.

THE BASQUE PELOTA

The Basque people have a fierce independence so even though distinct regions of the Basque country are ruled by both French and Spanish governments, they tend to do their own thing. The history of jai alai speaks to this independence. While the French were developing their form of clay-court tennis on red clay (originally stained red due to cattle blood), the Basques over the Pyrenees from France and beyond Andorra developed a series of different games [4]. French tennis balls at that time were called pelotes and were made of wool or string that was wound tightly, with a leather cover sewn over that. The Basques originally used rubber or gutta-percha as the core, sometimes wrapping it with wool and sewing it together with leather. With that, la pelota (Spanish for "ball") was born. Several different games evolved from the use of these pelotas. One can use their hands to play a variant of hand-ball, or tools can be used to impact the ball, leading to different games that include a paddle (pala) and the punta cesta (more on this later), which led to jai alai [3].

The jai alai pelota is considered the most lethal ball of any sport. It's ¾ the size of a baseball, harder than a golf ball, and can travel upwards of 180 mph in a match (Guinness World Records has called it "the world's fastest ball"[5]). Today's modern pelota is hand constructed using a hard core and two goat-skin covers. La pelota is a hand-wrapped and stitched leather ball that has gum, rosin or other elastomer included to make it bounce. Every 125-140g pelota is made a little differently by a few skilled craftsmen,—but every ball is unique. Olatz Gonzalez-Abrisketa mentioned to Brian that there is a burgeoning company in the Basque region that has built two custom machines to create a more standardized ball, but there's no machine built to construct an official pelota. No two pelotas are the same.

Playing with a ball that undergoes such extreme deformation is another challenge. The impact of the ball hitting a granite wall time and time again creates a lot of hysteresis loading on the ball. The compression and resilience of the ball tend to heat it up. If the pelota warms up during the match, the ball makes a distinctively less elastic sound. There's often a need to re-cover/restitch balls to maintain them as part of match play. If the ball lasts a match, it's commonly stored for a month to allow it to recover its original elasticity [1]. The deformation induced heating also means that the rebound restitution of the ball changes during the game based on its temperature.

THE BASQUE CESTA

In jai alai, the ball is hurled from a tool called a punta cesta—a horn-shaped device that has a radius of curvature of about 12 inches. Mark Kurlansky states that the original cesta dates back to 1857, invented by a young potato farmer in Saint Pée named Gantxiki Harotcha who used baskets for scooping up vegetables [4].

From those early days, the basic cesta was reshaped into what was called a xistera to catch and release la pelota. It incorporated a fixed glove so that the player could use centripetal force to catch, release, and accelerate the ball back to the wall. Melchor Guruceaga, an Argentinian Basque pelota player, is actually credited in the 1900s with adapting the xistera with some minor changes and adaptations to allow him to play with an arm injury [3]. His adaptations led to the basic design of the modern jai alai punta cesta used for the most part today.

The cesta fits over the arm of the player and each player uses the curvature of the cesta to create centripetal force. Good players can easily fling la pelota out of the cesta at more 110 mph, hence the other critical need for a jai alai player is a helmet to prevent getting hit by said pelota ricocheting off of the wall.

French postal stamp shows men with cestas attached; circa 1956. *Credit: Shutterstock*

THE GAME OF JAI ALAI

Jai alai can be played one-on-one by teams comprised of as many as eight players, or as a team sport of 2-on-2. Jai alai is historically played outside on promenades at dedicated arenas for spectators in and around Spain. The popularity of the sport took off and there were successful facilities formed in Cuba and Mexico and from there throughout a lot of South America. Outside of Europe, there are dedicated fronton buildings built in North America and other sites, to accommodate weather or to control access.

Basque pelota cesta punta player. *Credit: Shutterstock*

The best-preserved promenade facility is in Madrid [6, 7]. The jai alai court is a three-sided rectangular box with three solid and playable sides and a single open, screened, or walled off glass side where spectators can watch and bet accordingly.

There's a front wall, a back wall and a third wall in play on the left side, but none on the right. All jai alai players are required to hurl the ball with the cesta on their right arm. As they toss the ball, their momentum tends to keep them in front of the wall and in play. As a result, there are no left-handed cestas available and it's written into the rules that the cesta has to be on the right hand. Of course, if the teams played against the back wall, the same things would apply for left-handed cesta hurlers, but often the front and back walls are made from different materials. The bottom line is *NO left handed hurling.* To survive the large momentum impacts, granite is the most common material for the front facing wall.

Looking opposite the fronton wall at Fronton el Beti Jai, Madrid, published in El Peloton magazine, November 29, 1894.

Jai alai is played in a variety of formats. Friendly matches look a lot like racquetball or squash where singles of pairs square off and the scoring is similar. One team serves and the receiving player or players collect the ball, and, in one consistent motion, fling it back against the wall. This repeats back and forth until someone wins a point.

Points are won when the ball bounces out of bounds, the receiving team is unable to collect the ball either on the fly or after a single bounce, or if the throwing player is deemed to not use a single continuous motion in hurling la pelota back to the wall. Referees regulate the game to determine what constitutes a fluid motion, what is a catch, what is considered a foul serve, etc.

If jai alai is played like racquetball or squash, it's usually described as a "set" format. The goal in set play is to win a prescribed number of points (11, or 15 informally, the classic Basque sets go 35 points), which constitute one set. Winning a match looks like tennis in that one has to win a best two out of three sets or some similar format.

Probably the most common scoring format and the one most amenable for gambling is a round-robin, consisting of eight teams, either singles or pairs. In the round robin format, team one plays team two. When one of those teams wins a point, the losing team is sent off and the winning team stays on the court and faces off with team three, where those teams duel for another point and so on. The team that scores seven points wins. A common variant is what is called Spectacular Seven scoring in which points double after each team has won at least one point. This tends to make it easier for any one team to reach seven points and raises the pressure on leading teams to get back onto the court and trailing teams to keep them off the court altogether.

Each player or team is numbered 1-8 like horses in horse racing. We're sure there are handicapping books on who plays better where and when, and exotic bets that the spectator can put on who will win, and who finishes second, etc., like the exacta and trifecta wagering in horse racing.

With few functioning jai alai venues still in operation, it's easier to study how home field advantage might work there. If the players are free agents and move between frontons, then each time they play at a new fronton, they're playing with pelotas produced typically by the house. As pelotas are handmade, there may be some regularity within a fronton, but less between them. This suggests that those players more likely to win have played with the house pelotas before. The players work for themselves and are hired by a home fronton or house for matches. Unlike many professional sports with a union in place to negotiate on their behalf, jai alai players deal with the frontons as individuals, which is what helped trigger the original spat in the late 1980s about pay, insurance, and performance incentives.

As the game of jai alai expanded from St Pee to many other Basque cities, the fronton was prominently situated [4] in the center of town as a meeting place and a kind of plaza. As such, each fronton seems to have different dimensions, which carried into today's version of the game (see table of existing dimensions of viable frontons in the US). Additionally, each fronton was constructed from different materials which in due time probably affected the roughness of the wall and rebound angles of balls bouncing off.

Pictures of the original open-air fronton in Madrid showing the players on the left and the spectators on the right, with acknowledgment and permission from the Salvemos el Fronton Beti Jai Madrid and photographed by a photographer named Duque. Published in El Peloton magazine, November 29, 1894.

These wall variations would again give players who had more experience at the same fronton more of an advantage in terms of funny angles, dead spots in the floor, etc. Finally, the schemes for collusion between those who were playing, and those making the equipment probably added to the leverage for those wagering on games played. Bottom line, have a grand time watching jai alai, bet a little, and enjoy the show.

Fronton	Location	Length	Width	Overhead Dimensions (in feet)	Status	Operational Since
Miami	South FL	176ft	45ft	40	Year round	1920s
Ocala	Central FL	176	40	45	Seasonal	1973
Ft Pierce	South FL	176	50	40	Seasonal	1974
Orlando	Central FL	180	50	48	Seasonal	1962
Dania	South FL	178	50	45	Year round	1953

Features of operational jai alai frontons in the United States. [8]

DON'T TELL JOKES WHILE SPEEDSKATING. THE ICE MIGHT CRACK UP!

SOFIA, Bulgaria: Wang Meng of China competes in the women's 1000 meters short track speed skating at the Samsung ISU World Cup on February 8, 2009. *Credit: Shutterstock*

THE HISTORY OF SKATING

Skating dates back thousands of years and was limited to the frozen climates of northern Europe, Scandinavia, and other arctic terrains. UK researcher Federico Formenti, part sports physiologist and part archeologist, compared the performance of historical recreations of various skating systems going back as far as 1800 BC to the 17th century [9]. With deep snow and lakes freezing over, some means of traversing frozen space was required. Pioneers strapped bones to their shoes and used them to glide across frozen lakes and streams. Already well into the iron age, it was just a matter of time until iron-based skates were developed, first as attachments to shoes and then incorporated into shoe designs. Since the development of the International Skating Union in the middle 1800s[10], the sport has remained rather similar in both look and performance.

The evolution of ice resurfacing machines and HVAC systems for indoor facilities has improved ice consistency and flatness, making the process of skating more standardized. Certain body and shoe attributes were linked to peak performances and the Dutch and the Scandina-vians with tall, lean bodies and long legs seemed to have an edge over other skaters. Speedskaters generally look similar with long loping strides over long straightaways and a skate over skate stride in the curves of oval skating rinks. One arm is tucked behind one's back while the other dangles in a controlled toggle with each stride. Smaller skaters have to raise their cadence to compete. Skater efficiency separates the medalists from the also-rans.

While an even longer skating blade might increase contact time with the ice surface, the blade required strength to lift the skate off the ice surface. Too big a blade can be somewhat cumbersome making it difficult not to hit the other skate in the turns. Bodies got bigger, and aerobic training helped certain skaters increase their cadence to increase their velocity across the surface. Drag has been reduced by rubber skating suits that not only provide thermal insulation when gliding at 30mph but reduce turbulent drag when more loose clothing fluttered in the wind.

THE EVOLUTION OF MODERN SKATES

The sport of speed skating evolved while technical advancements occurred in training, aerobic conditioning, clothing, and field surface conditioning. There were technical achievements in the development of new skating technology, but they were cumbersome and challenging to get established speed skaters to adopt. A German technologist named Karl Hannes developed a hinged or detachable skate that allowed more free movement of the feet while still being connecting to the blade apparatus, (German Patent # DE 78733, approved in 1894).

Surprisingly, it took nearly 100 years of tinkering, tweaking, and cajoling for skaters to consider using the alternative skate, and how

much that paid off was unimaginable. The largest contribution came from, of course, another Dutchman named Gerrit Jan van Ingan Schenau who studied the biomechanics of propulsion linked with speed skating [1, 2]. In the process of producing his dissertation, he found that the ankle was not fully extended in speed skating with a fixed skate as was observed with running. The lack of extension led to incomplete propulsion as compensation for the fixed blade, which led him to the same conclusion as Mr. Hannes 80 years earlier. This led to some alternative designs and new prototypes, with a spring action hinge mechanisms to allow the shoe to flex with the blade contacting the ice longer during each stride. This invention was known as the clap skate. The

Men's speed skater competition showing clap skate. *Credit: Shutterstock*

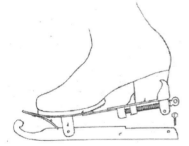

DE 78733, the German Hannes patent linked with a decoupled skate, January 26, 1894.

biomechanics suggested that a more effective ankle extension that should increase the efficiency it had in skating propulsion.

The proof was in the pudding as a first few pioneer skaters learned how to use the skates and leverage this new boot flexibility. For a period of five years between the Lillehammer and Nagano Olympics in 1994 and 1998, speed-skating records fell extensively. In Lillehammer, only five world speedskating records were produced out of the 10 events between the men's and women's 500m, 1,000m, 1,500m, 5K and 10K races. With clap skates more widely accepted, new records were established in nine races, with the only record that didn't fall tied in Nagano. In the women's 5,000m race, it took five years to break the world record established in 1988, and over the next five years with clapskates, it was broken four additional times.

The countour of the speed skate has no toe prong as with a figure skate. *Credit: Shutterstock*

The following figure corresponds to how the world record for the women's 5,000m has evolved showing time in seconds [3]. The confluence of better training and better athletes saw an early drop-off in record times, but the progressive drop in times was due to new skaters mastering the clap skates. Chances are that now that the entire elite segment of the sport has transitioned to clap skates, there will be further refinements in skate design that will result in even faster times. The current record holder in the 5,000m is Martina Sablikova, a Czech skater who finished in 6 minutes and 42 seconds, in February 2011 and was not challenged in either the Sochi or Pyeongchang Olympics [3]. That's 12.4 meters/second or 27.7 mph.

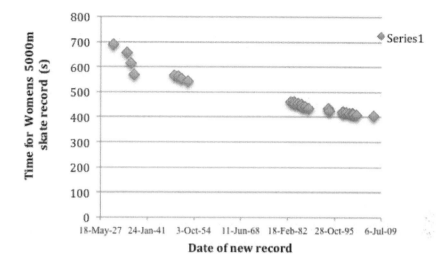

SHORT TRACK

While speedskaters are typically tall, they have incredible lower body strength as well. Now that they're equipped with clap skates, there's been a revolution in other types of ice skating like short track—which looks more like roller derby on ice. In short track, completely different body types thrive and clap skates have been outlawed. In short track, a small group of four skaters race at a time around an oval track that is mostly curved. The track is 200 feet long end-to-end and 98 feet wide —the same dimensions as an international hockey rink [7]. The skaters typically never use the whole track trying to shave off distance by staying as close to the inside as possible. Traditional speedskating has two skaters on the ice at a time, and there's a decorum on how to avoid each other on the track to avoid collisions and contact.

In short track, it's a race of 500 or 1,000 meters, with all sorts of jockeying for position. Collisions, contact, and skating in someone's space is compulsory if you want to be competitive in short track, the antithesis of conventional speed skating. Rules and disqualifications exist for flagrant fouls but if someone wipes out in front of you and takes you with them in short track, that's part of the game, making short track a little ragged. The best comparison is NASCAR—a bunch of left turns and a lot of rubbing—though in short track there aren't any pit stops.

The strategy in short track, unlike speedskating, is not about absolute time. Each racer is racing ultimately against others. To win and medal in short track, one needs to be in the final race of racers at any distance. To get there requires passing through qualification heats and usually the top 2 are taken in each of these. Wiping out in an early heat or not finishing in the top 2 is tantamount to ending one's chance at medaling.

CULTIVATING TALENT FROM OTHER SPORTS TO LEVERAGE IN SHORT TRACK SKATING

Like bobsleigh, Olympic speedskating programs have increasingly looked at summer Olympians and elite sprinters to produce faster teams and results—scouring outdoor skate parks and beyond to look for inline roller blade skaters who have mastered the idea of skating, just not on ice. A number of converts from wheels to ice include Apolo Ohno and Erin Johnson, and looking for skaters from skate parks has helped to democratize the sport a little in the U.S. [4[6]]. Short track has also created new opportunities for figure skaters who don't fit the mold, or are either too fast or not particularly good fits for the rigor required to thrive in either singles or pairs figure skating. Add Maame Biney, [5] a Ghanian-American figure skater turned short-track icer in that crowd.

Inline skating might be able to make a compelling case for being added as an Olympic sport. There are a variety of international competitions, reasonable interest certainly on par with track and field, and a growing crop of inline skaters who compete. It may well be that the imbalance between the large number of summer events relative to winter events at the Olympics and the stark reality that speedskating gets better if drawing from a larger pool of potential skaters might lead to the reality that to go to the Olympics, many inline skates have had to transition to ice skates to compete for their country. [8]

World record performances occur at the intersection of good training, an ideal skater in terms of physical dimensions and strength, advanced equipment and clothing, confidence and some luck. Having all the intangibles doesn't necessarily guarantee peak performance, but there's more chance of a better outcome. Continued assaults on world records will continue as skaters get physically stronger, master clap skates more completely, and designers work to optimize future skate designs for the most effortless performance.

STICKS AND STONES AND FRIGID ICE

Curling

SVETLOGORSK, Russia: Belarussian team members curl during IX International Medexpert Curling Cup, August, 5, 2017. *Credit: Shutterstock*

C urling is one of those funny sports embraced by cold weather countries that leave a lot of Americans scratching their heads every four years during the Winter Olympics. In the interim, regular competitions called bonspiels are held in relative obscurity except in these curling-crazy countries. The largest competitions in Canada are the men's and women's national tournaments, where teams representing provinces square off against each other and the National Team. If a provincial team wins the national championship, they become the National Team. If it's an Olympic year, a separate competition is held between Team Canada and other teams with the winning team that represents Canada in curling that year. Professional curlers don't make enough money (even National Team players) to survive, so they also tend to be bookkeepers, insurance agents, and take other day jobs while curling.

CURLING: SHUFFLEBOARD POETRY IN MOTION

Curling might seem like a slow or unappealing sport but there's a tremendous level of strategy. It takes power, grace, and a functional awareness of kinematics to be successful. The transactions executed in curling require players to slide a stone across a sheet of ice to a scoring zone. The sliding is called tossing or throwing the stone, but that stone weighs three times more than a bowling ball, so there isn't much tossing going around. Once the sliding starts, teammates use brooms to contour the ice and direct the stone to a scoring area downrange from where the toss occurs. When executed well, curling looks effortless and subtle. There's a lot of team communication to gauge how fast the stone is sliding, where they want the stone to go, and often a lot of yelling.

Curling is like shuffleboard on ice. Picture a series of concentric rings as a target some 120-130 feet away. The innermost bullseye is called the button—four feet in diameter. There are concentric annuli two-feet wide that create a 12-foot circle where teams try to put the curling stones (the rocks). The concentric ring formation is called the house.

Four players make up a team—the skip, the third, the second (or vice skip), and lead, usually throwing in opposite order. Two teams compete against each other on a single sheet of ice (they don't call it a rink). Each player gets two stones to slide down to the target area, while their teammates sweep the ice equipped with brooms. Players alternate throwing back and forth until all 16 stones are tossed in what's called an end. Scoring is addressed at the conclusion of each end, and teams start over, tossing everything back to the target on the other side of the sheet for a new end. There are 10 ends in curling that are like innings in baseball.

The goal is to get the stones (the rocks) into the scoring zone (the house). *Credit: Shutterstock*

WHAT MAKES A CURLING STONE?

The best curling stones are mined from one of two granite mines in the world—an island called Ailsa Craig near Kays, Scotland, that's been operational since 1851 and produces about two-thirds of the world's stones (another third come from a Welsh mine). The Kays Curling Club has the sole lease to mine granite from the Ailsa Craig quarry. Since the island became a bird sanctuary in the 1990s, it took some time to iron out whether the island could still be mined for stone blanks [1]. In the interim, there were efforts to produce stone sliding inserts as updates for reconditioned stones.

Rough stones of blue-hone granite are polished and shaped and a handle is attached to maintain a 38-44-pound nominal weight (most are 42 lbs). Blue hone stone is particularly good for curling with a low water absorption rate, making it less susceptible to freeze/thaw-induced cracking during long-term play. Stones last about 100 years. The density of the stones collected from the Ailsa Craig are uniform, so all the stones with the same dimensions have the same stone mass.

PUTTING THE CURL IN CURLING

Curling sheets aren't mirrored finishes but feature small particles of ice that impart some level of micro-roughness and texture on the surface. Modern ice resurfacing machines are capable of spitting out freezing pebbles of ice along with the freezing water that provides some texture to an otherwise flat surface of ice.

A small twist of the stone as it's tossed, thrown, or slid from one end to the house, will cause the stone to spin as it slides over the textured ice pebbles. More twist yields more spin and more bend. That's where the sport's name comes from—curling stones for tactical advantage.

The decision of how much twist to apply leads to a variety of outcomes as described by Joe Murphy, managing director of the Train Smart for Curling Program in Canada, who also coached the Newfoundland and Labrador provincial teams that competed in the 2018 National Curling Championship. Too much rotation will overcome all of the friction on the ice and cause the stone to go mostly straight. Too slow a spin and the stone bobs and weaves a little bit like a knuckleball. Ideal spin and velocity lead to a stone that slides straight initially and, as it slows, bends thanks to the texture of the ice. Players can twist the stone clockwise or counterclockwise to allow the thrower to bend the stone left or right. It doesn't matter much when the first stone is being thrown, but after five stones are near the house, it's increasingly important to be able to bend the directionality of the stones for more precise play. One hears the refrain "putting the rock in the house" which means trying to put the stone in the scoring zone. Here's where curling brooms come into play.

STICKS AND STICKLERS

It would be a rather uninvolved game if each player tossed their stones while their three teammates watched. Tossing the stone is actually the first step in a beautiful coordinated dance between the thrower, the sweepers, and usually the skip—to direct the sweepers as to how much and where to sweep to yield an appropriate amount of curl. The thrower usually times their shot based on how fast it's moving and the sweepers hover over the moving stone and sweep or hold tight. The sweeper's job is to sweep away the asperities of micro-roughness on the ice surface and provide friction to alter how far the stone moves. A hard throw is called a weight shot and is designed to clear rocks from the scoring zone and usually doesn't require a lot of sweeping. More finesse shots behind other stones in the scoring section require a more delicate throw and more coordination amongst the team to bend the rotating stone behind other stones. Many shots require some physics to accommodate the carom and rebound from rocks that collide. Brooms for sweeping were originally taken from home closets, made from straw, and were generally effective when curling was played outside where snow fell on already formed sheets of ice.

Within the last 50 years, curlers angling for an edge have experienced a revolution in new types of abrasive surfaces for brooms, from horsehair and hoghair bristles to nylon and other abrasive sponges attached to broom poles. The poles are now made from fiberglass and carbon fiber reinforced composite that are lighter and allow for more force to be applied. As far as the business end of the broom goes, the new rage is directional fabric that is more effective at abrading the surface and increasing the amount of friction [3]. You run out there with your Swiffer, and by altering the roughness of the head, you're affecting the number and depth of grooves being formed in the ice just in front of the trailing stone. By controlling the texture of the abrasion surface by using different sized yarns, these directional fabrics function more like files or rasps and less like a broad abrasive sponge. Applied to ice, grooves cut in the pebbles and the ice surface have a larger degree of control on the amount of curl achieved [4].

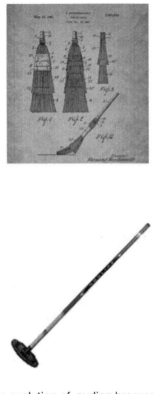

The evolution of curling brooms, from early horsehair brooms (F Marchessault, US Patent # 2983939, issued May 16th, 1961) to engineered foams, fabrics, and brushes.

The issues with the new broom technology were revolutionary enough to generate questions within the community during the Sochi Olympics about whether these new more potent sweepers were actually illegal. Curling is a rather unkempt sport and there are no written requirements or rules about the specific type of broom, material, texture, or other attributes of brooms. At least for Sochi, a number of teams volunteered to skip using the high tech brooms.

BROOMGATE

John Cullen, a 20-year curler and stand-up comic from Vancouver [6] told us a story known in curling circles as Broomgate [7]. Most equipment companies supporting the curling industry have been helped by elite curlers who've collaborated and participated in new product design to help the rest of the sport. There was some understanding that these engineered, directional fabrics scratching the surface led to a more responsive and controllable curl, but elite curlers were only playing around with these new brooms.

Soon, there were a few players sporting brooms with what were called icePads, from a company out of Montreal called Hardline. The players using these were hardly considered elite, but they played well using the brooms. It was as if the throw of the rock no longer mattered, as terrific sweeping made up for many throwing sins. Brad Gushue, one of the elite players in the sport, told NPR it was becoming difficult to miss a shot with these newly engineered brooms.

Cullen mentioned that some teams were upset that the technology was eclipsing the skill elements of the sport. It was as if the sweeper could scrub the surface of the ice and lay down a magnetic track which would guide the stone wherever the thrower wanted it to go, and it was aptly referred to as "joystick" sweeping. Competitive teams figured out that it was better to have only one sweeper than two, and this single sweeper with the engineered broom could have a strong influence to direct exactly how a thrown stone could be bent around other stones, etc. The World Curling Federation took notice of the concerns and held a summit testing a range of new brooms and engineered surfaces with both curlers and scientists [7]. Their recommendation was to allow these engineered brooms to be used in recreational play but not for sanctioned events. The federation also made reference to the fact that in competition the broom heads needed to be commercially available to all teams and could not be doctored by the team.

ROMANCING THE STONE

What's amazing to consider is stone management. Most clubs own their own stones and put them out on the ice for tournament play. Tournaments also own their own sets of rocks. The stones are periodically checked for damage and are commonly turned once a year on a polishing/grinder to address wear and abrasion. Sanctioned events actually fly their rocks around if the tournament moves from one venue to another like the Scotties. You come back a year later to play at the same venue or tournament and get some of the same stones you played with the year before. There might be subtleties in how each stone curls, whether it feels lighter, etc. These stones are marked with designators and so it's possible to do some analytics on how your team executed with each of the eight rocks used.

The discipline for tracking rock performance is buried in charts and notebooks. At the elite level, players take the time to log every stone to note its propensity to bend, slide faster, or behave erratically. Some teams go for the Zen of the moment and grab whatever stone is near them. Others like famous curler Kevin Martin kept a legendary rock book managed by Jules Owchar in which all details of every stone were noted—although it's hard to think of a wins over replacement strategy for the stones—only players [2]. Stones last so long that it's possible a well-kept rock book could get quite extensive. When Kevin Martin retired from competitive curling, Owchar's acquired knowledge was picked up by Glenn Howard, also an elite curler and technowonk who loved the analytical approach [2].

SLIP SLIDING AWAY

The whole curling enterprise is funny to watch, in part because players use two different shoes—a gripping surface on one that allows the player to retain their stability on the surface of the ice, and a second shoe called a slider that slides. By putting more force on the slider, players tossing the stone can glide across the ice before letting go of the stone. Moving back and forth between throwing and scoring zones, one is required to glide on the slider, push with the gripper, and glide again.

It's amazing to see adept players slide along, avoid contact with stones in play, and still sweep as they go. Even elite players can't avoid every rock while sliding, and some suffered errant stumbles. In 2015, at the Master's Grand Slam of Curling, skip Brad Gushue was standing in the house as one of his teammates was throwing a stone and as the stone reached the house, Gushue stepped away, only to slip and fall face-first onto the ice. He was patched up by the medical staff and played the last ends of the match. In the interim, his team hobbled along playing with only three players, common if someone gets injured. Helmets are available to players, along with other less intrusive head-gear, and even padded donut shaped headbands called ice halos [5] for the more fashion conscious.

It's always possible that sweepers will bump a stone as they're sweeping and sliding, resulting in what's called a burnt stone—a foul that results in a series of actions to reestablish play. There is some discretion among the non-offending team as to whether to return stones to the rough positions they were situated before the foul, remove stones altogether, or leave things as the rested after the foul. Officials oversee contests, but it's expected that they're only there for measurements and, to a lesser extent, to act as arbiters if conflicts can't be settled amongst the players.

One can imagine that what was originally a relatively inexpensive sport with duct tape to make a sliding shoe, a broom taken from home, a decent winter jacket and some liquid insulation, one could curl quite economically. But as new technology seeps in and as the wardrobe has expanded to include some pretty stylish pants, the cost to play has increased quite a bit. Curling hasn't caught on in the U.S., except a few weeks every four years when we tune in to observe this funny sport that deserves more attention and respect. Curling is really a form of applied physics—more interesting than billiards.

We're waiting for the next skip named Saskatoon Fats.

WAX ON, WAX OFF

The Mechanics of Modern Skiing

| Credit: Shutterstock

The word skiing derives from the Norwegian word, skiŏ, which translates to split piece of wood [1]. From those humble origins of strapping sticks to one's shoes, skiing has developed into an international sport with events like slalom, downhill, and cross country skiing, as well as integrated sports such as biathlon.

Many of the timed events date back to the first modern winter Olympics held in 1924 in Chamonix, France, a lovely little hamlet on the border with Italy that now can be accessed by a gondola [2]. New variations like freestyle skiing, ski-cross, and snowboarding on the half-pipe have arrived as hybrids from the X-Games and other crossover sports. These new events use judges and style points—the antithesis of the timed sports.

THE ETYMOLOGY OF SKIING

The word slalom comes from the Norwegian word "slalåm" which means sloping track [6]. The word gondola—the air trams that convey skiers to the slopes—traces its origins to late 16th century Venice. Relating to skiing, references were found in the late 19th century by an Italian futurist who described aerial ships that could be used in the future to convey skiers, 300 years hence [7]. Apparently it didn't take that long. Skiers are also conveyed by tow ropes, ski lifts or by the French word funiculaire, derived from the Latin word finiculus for cord or umbilical cord—a track- or rail-based tram pulled by a cord for propulsion [8].

Freshly packed snow trails often show a kind of a grooved pattern representative or corduroy pants, hence the name corduroy trail. Before the funicular and the gondola, skiers had to herringbone their way up hills, splaying their skis outward and making a series of hops to increase in altitude as you go. It's common to observe this with cross-country skiers using the herringbone technique to maintain their speed and not lose momentum. Everything has a fish analogy in Sweden and Norway. Of course there's always the face plant which is self-explanatory, and if everything falls off of you during an epic face plant, that is called a garage sale—to suggest broken skis, poles, and perhaps bones [9].

| Credit: Shutterstock

ROSIN BRAN

It didn't take long to figure out in Scandinavia, centuries before the Olympics, that wooden sticks as skis absorbed a lot of water, making them heavier, less stiff, slower, and more difficult to use [2]. By drying and waterproofing the wood used to make skis—usually with a sealant applied—immediate benefits were recognized, not only for the longevity of the skis but also in terms of performance. Some of the original sealants were derived from the rendering of wood scraps that were burned very slowly to make charcoal and a wood rosin extract that included a pine tar called pitch [3]. The pine tar and rosin could be applied as goo or resin over the edges of the wood and with sufficient drying, the result was a layer that not only reduced moisture penetration but enhanced the sliding performance of the ski. Resin deposition was hardly flat to begin with, and newer dispensing systems improved the evenness of the coating. The resins lowered the coefficient of friction of the ski encountering snow and by flexing the ski, the asperities of the coating would help the ski grip the surface on turns.

Pine tar is very sticky and difficult to work with. The notion of using something easier to dispense is appealing. Ski resurfacers started using hydrophobic paraffin waxes as alternatives. Waxes are essentially

20-30 carbon length hydrocarbons that melt at temperatures of 50-70°C and crystallize into solid forms above room temperature. At temperatures below freezing, where most skiing occurs, waxes solidify rather hard and are very hydrophobic. Another feature of sliding surfaces, regardless of the wax, is that the coefficient of friction regulates how much frictional heating occurs as the skier slides across the snow surface.

The coefficient of friction is a physics term. Consider a skier who stands on his/her skies. They have a certain body mass and gravity is pushing the skier into the mountain with a certain normal force. To ski is to propel one's body using poles as a force perpendicular to the normal force. The force preventing you from sliding is the friction of your shoe or ski surfaces relative to the mountain and you have to push with your poles to overcome that force. The coefficient of friction is a ratio of how much your normal force conveys into a frictional force. A high coefficient of friction requires a lot of energy to slide, and the heavier you are, the more force is required. A smaller coefficient of friction and one is slipping and sliding all over the place. Factors that regulate the amount of frictional force include the coefficient of friction, the relative roughness of the ski and snow surfaces, and the contact areas of the skis and the mass of the skier. That same skier who eats a meal or drinks a hot cocoa has a slightly higher frictional force since there is a higher normal force operating with that same coefficent of friction. Frictional heating occurs between the surfaces as sliding ensues. A ski continuously sliding across a snow surface causes the outermost layer of wax in contact with the snow to warm up. The longer the skier skis, the warmer the wax gets. If the wax gets warm enough to melt, it can slide off the ski, leaving wax on the slope and a diminishing amount on the ski as the skier progresses downhill. If the ablation rate of the wax is sufficiently high, it's possible that the wax can be completely worn off before the skier finishes his/her race.

There are all sorts of details of the contact mechanics of a sliding multi-layer ski on either ice or powdered snow, and there are different mechanisms of *lubrication* that regulate ultimately how much energy is dissipated when a ski slides so far. For example, if the powder compresses or compacts while the skier skis downhill, that can change the mechanics. Similarly, it the combination of force and friction melts a thin layer of water between the ski and ice, that mechanism is called *squeeze film lubrication*. If the wax melts and sloughs off while the skier skis downhill, that's another lubrication mechanism. And similarly, if there are particulates in the snow like dirt or hard ice crystals, those can scratch the surfaces of the skies and alter how much the skis slide. That is called a 3-body wear example, the ski, the snow and the dirt all affect the contact mechanics. All of these mechanisms are temperature dependent and the friction generated can change temperature even more, making skiing a dynamic process. The plethora of lubrication schemes is so vast as to be beyond this book's capacity to describe lubrication mechanisms that govern all skiing. Suffice it to say that different lubrication models might all be relevant in specific cases, and maybe that's the rationale for the myriad of goos, waxes, and rosins used to enhance lubrication.

TYPES OF SKI COMPETITIONS

There are long and short ski races. The shortest races are performed by ski jumpers, and they're not really races at all. Skiers slide down a long chute, are propelled off the mountain, and try to land. Most of their trip downhill is through the air. Ski jumpers might be sliding on snow surfaces less than 20 seconds per jump. Sprint races include the downhill and slalom, where skiers traverse downhill nearly a full mountain achieving speeds of more than 50 mph in the process. Each of those races takes about two minutes.

Endurance races like cross-country and the biathlon tend to progress rather slowly without the aid of gravity pushing the downhill skiers down the mountain. The typical distances covered are as long as 50 km, and these races are executed over periods between about 10 minutes for sprints or as much as two hours for marathon distances.

Higher speed races are more abrasive to the waxes but they are obviously much shorter. With the development of longer chain hydrocarbon and fluorocarbon solid waxes, these coatings tend to melt at higher temperatures so they're more likely to resist ablation and erosion due to frictional heating as a skier slides. It's also possible that the long chain wax molecules, experiencing a shear force due to the sliding, align in the direction of the shear, which also tends to reduce the coefficient of friction in the chain alignment direction. Thus, it's actually possible that a ski glides the bottom of the mountain more easily than at the top, and it's possible that conditioning the skis results in a lower friction coating assuming it doesn't melt and doesn't abrade. Wax coatings can be damaged by sliding on a more abrasive surface (think sandpaper). The wear and impact damage on ski coatings and waxes can also be experienced by aerialists, although any subtle change in the abrasive characteristics of the snow probably affects the cross-country skiers even more.

Since the first wooden skis were developed, a revolution in ski design has occurred for the complete customization of the ski. This includes the dimensions, curvature, boot integration, and ski stiffness that all contribute to the selection of what someone is ultimately strapped into. Once those selections are made, there's a continued refinement of what kind of sliding surface is desired. Included in this selection is the type of dispenser, the thickness of the coating, and whether to distribute an even thickness over the whole ski or gradients in coating thickness. There are differences in wax composition and that can also affect the coefficient of friction. With the proliferation of ski waxes and dispensing technologies, the technical details in preparing skiers to perform at the elite level have expanded and with those has come a much larger support staff behind each elite skier. In addition to the direct waxing efforts, other activities include trial and error, scout ski tests, and embedded knowledge from prior experiences.

RECENT OLYMPICS SKIING LORE

The two most recent Winter Olympics were held in Russia in 2014 and South Korea in 2018. The temperatures during the Olympics in Sochi, Russia were 3°C, but the presence of the sun on the sunny side of the slopes caused a lot of snow melt from trees, creating frozen icy/slushy conditions on the trails [4]. The formation of the slush was more apparent after 2 p.m. when many of the races were scheduled. A softer waxed ski might perform perfectly at 11:30 a.mm but erode much faster at 2:30 p.m.

A lesson learned was that waxers needed to be much closer to the skiers to make any last minute adjustments in waxing strategy. This wasn't possible for the Canadian and Norwegian cross-country skiers in Sochi. These two teams underperformed relative to their usual times, mainly by the selection of waxes that melted in the warmer conditions and they were stuck with and an inability to opt for a different choice. One can compare the wet and hot conditions in Sochi with the much more unforgiving cold in Pyeongchang, South Korea, which had conditions regularly at -20 C. At these temperatures, ice tended to freeze near the tips of the skis, which abraded the waxes that were being used [5]. All waxers have a plan B and the pathway to forming much harder waxes led to more optimum performance. So the waxes, the thickness, and ultimately the conditions of the course regulate the selection and the strategy of how to wax.

What's interesting is that there's no real comparison between one Olympics and another, except for the cross-country races. One downhill course is different from the rest, and as individual performances, there are nuances that can favor one skier over another. One has to appreciate the individual performances for what they are. Sometimes racing later vs earlier in the day can bias how well a skier performs. Performing in a blizzard might be dramatically different in terms of clearly seeing the race course than under pristine conditions. Skiing under clouds might be different than skiing in the glare of a sunny reflecting ski slope.

Today, there are hundreds of ski waxes to choose from, leading to decisions about how much wax, what type, and under what conditions one is skiing. Wax selection and deposition decisions are made long before the casual skier rents a pair of skis at the backcountry ski shop. Chances are that most of those rental skiers wouldn't be aware of the distinctions between a high-quality and an inferior waxing job, but it could make all the difference.

MAKING WAVES IN THE DEEP END

Similar to the notion that clap skates improved the performance of speedskaters, the development of high tech contoured swimwear has resulted in dramatic assaults on the record books in the pool. For much of the modern era, up to 1990, the quest to improve efficiency in swimming centered on maximizing hand and foot size, stronger appendages, and more efficient breathing techniques. Large training emphases were placed on improving cardiovascular function. Elite swimmers possess most, if not all all, of these attributes.

Doping programs of the 1970s led to larger swimmers with larger lung capacity and larger muscles. That the testosterone-laced female swimmers looked more like men didn't result in sufficient controversy to disqualify swimmers until it was clear the size and scope of doping in eastern European training houses for swimmers. At the time, when it came to swimwear, it was thought that less suit was better, with less material being carried through the water.

GROW YOUR SWIMMER BIGGER ... POWER OVER DRAG

The prevailing thought up until 1990 was that power overcomes drag. The outside layer of skin is a porous structure through which hairs

ROME, Italy: Michael Phelps in the mens 100m butterfly final at the 13th Fina World Aquatics Championships held in the The Foro Italico Swimming Complex, July 1, 2009. *Credit: Shutterstock*

protrude and corneocytes—flattened, dehydrated keratinocytes—provide a barrier to pathogens. Exfoliating in the shower with a loofah sponge scrapes off those outer layers of skin cells. Shaving or waxing the skin creates less drag in the pool as well.

Those skin cells have a characteristic surface energy. When water contacts the skin surface, it beads up, since water has a higher surface energy than the skin layer. Everyone has about the same composition of skin, assuming every swimmer shaves to reduce drag. A bigger swimmer has more propulsion capacity but also more surface area to act as a drag force.

Fast-forward to the Olympics of 1992 where disruptive thinking evolved on how swimsuits could be designed to enhance performance. The process of forming fabrics with more contour to create smoother profiles in the water was already evident. The thought to expand the coverage area of suits from neck to ankle certainly made swimmers more contoured. Advanced swimsuits possessed a closed cell porosity that not only created a more insulated swimmer, but led to a larger buoyant force, leaving more of the athlete out of the water gliding on top as opposed to being more fully immersed in the water [1]. The second skin also had a different surface tension with water depending on the material it was made from.

There's a lot of research on flow dynamics of a swimmer gliding through the water [2]. This is the realm of fluid dynamics and chemical engineering linked with pressures, drags, and fluid motion and flow. Broadly though, picture a swimmer as a blob moving through the water.

A swimmer is burning energy moving their arms and legs in coordinated motion to propel the swimmer forward. A smooth stroke creates less turbulence in the water, increasing their efficiency. There are geometric features about the swimmer that need to be considered. One is how much the swimmer is submerged into the water, and the other what is the surface area to volume element of the swimmer.

Women swimmers at the starting line before competition. *Credit: Shutterstock*

The swimmer propelling himself/herself through the water is retarded by having to displace the water around them. The water can flow over the swimmer, or can be moved orthogonally as a wave or a ripple. Depending on the presence of waves in the water, which cause perturbations beyond what happens in a stagnant pool. The higher the swimmer is positioned out of the pool by buoyancy, the lower the overall drag since less water requires displacement. Air is also being displaced, but the drag force required to move air around is a lot lower than that for water. Regardless of where a swimmer is situated in the pool, the geometry of the swimmer also matters. The drag force propelling the water would be different if we were spherical swimmers. Humans actually look more representative of cylinders propelling through the water, similar to whales, dolphins, seals, and penguins. Competitive front crawl sprinters swim at velocities as high as 3 meters per second (m/s). Elite endurance swimmers can maintain a velocity of 1 meter per second. Jump in the water and swim with an egg beater stroke creating a massive number of bubbles around and the entire stroke will be less efficient.

CAN HUMANS BE CONTOURED INTO BELUGA WHALES?

How can swimming attire improve performance? One could wear better goggles. The head pushing through the water with goggles on creates massive amounts of turbulence. By streamlining goggles and creating contours and pockets for a swimmer's hair, turbulence is minimized and the swimmer can move faster [3]. Picture streamlined helmets like elite bicyclists and you get the idea of how one could reduce their profile in the water. Couple biometric data with the ability to 3D print their own low profile goggles and one can see how personalizing one's profile while swimming is readily available on an experimental basis today.

Once the head is resolved, the entire suit can be contoured so that the body looks more like a tube and less like a human. Aquatic animals like seals, beluga whales, and dolphins look like cylinders with tapered ends for the head and tail sections. Compression suits are designed to compress the hips, butt and chest, making a swimmer less hourglass shaped. These suits, often referred to as Fastskin or LZR label suits, are examples of how the contouring alone can alter swimmer efficiency [4].

Another method is to modify suit architecture and weaving to raise the buoyancy of the swimmer. Anything to reduce how much water the swimmer is displacing should result in less drag—meaning that they don't have to work as hard to achieve the same swim velocity. There are plenty of wet suits that simply contain a closed cell foam structure to provide air pockets within the suit to lift the swimmer higher out of the water. Foam features in these suits are the equivalent of swimming in the Dead Sea, where the higher salinity makes the water more dense and pushes more of you out of the water. The extra buoyancy has little to do with skin friction and more to do with the pressure drag.

If the surface of the suit was more hydrophobic, water would be repelled from the surface, creating less intimate contact with the water surface. It makes it easier for the suit to have a bigger air gap while sliding the suit through the water. Air pockets near the water/suit interface could drive down the frictional force between the swimmer and the water and lower the drag.

BETTER TRAINING AND TECHNOLOGY EQUALS IMPROVED PERFORMANCE

MILAN, Italy: Zsuzsanna Jakabos of Hungary in the Milan Swimming International Meeting on March 12, 2011. *Credit: Shutterstock*

Countless swimming records have fallen in the last 20 years since the development of contoured swimsuits. The rise in performance seemed to reach an inflection by the mid/late 1980s for both men and women, and continued improvements seem on a different slope based on work by Foster [5]. The impact has been profound—so much so that there have been efforts to forego high tech suits in lieu of more traditional suits that don't have the same features, or at least shrink the contact area from the belly button to the knee for men and from the shoulders to kneecaps for women [6]. There are now exacting details about what constitutes a regulation swimsuit, which includes details about how it's made and how it functions. For example, suits have to be a woven product, the cloth must be water permeable, and there are limitations on cloth buoyancy [7]. Further, once the suit is produced, NCAA rules prohibit the modification or alteration of the suit using water repellant sprays, oils, or tapes [7]. What was galling was that the best swimmers in the world were being neutralized by technology as opposed to letting actual swimming distinguish medal winners.

THE SHAPE OF THE POOL MATTERS

Competition natatoria have been increasingly engineered to reduce pool turbulence in an attempt to eke out further performance in the pool. This has been accomplished by engineering several different elements including the depth, the edge gratings, and the lane dimensions. Most competition pools are 3 meters deep. One could construct a deeper pool and the benefit of swimming in a deeper pool is that reflected waves created by a swimmer tend to be diminished compared to swimming in a much shallower pool. Swimming in a deeper pool can seem slower since one is farther away from fiducials or markings on the bottom of the pool. Swimming can also create transverse waves that typically emanate from the middle of the pool lanes where the fastest swimmers are located and radiate perpendicular to the swim direction.

At the outer edges of the pool on the perimeter, there are perimeter perimeter overflow gutters that can take waves from swimming and dissipate any reflection back into the pool. Furthermore, the dimensions of the lane can also be a pretty big influencer and they can be quite variable. Swimming rulebooks suggest a width larger than 7 feet and in collegiate pools, the lane width can be larger than 9 feet. In Olympic competition, the standard is 2.5 meters, and with 8 competing athletes in the pool, it is common that near the edges of the pool the outer two lanes are not used.. The swimmers lanes could be expanded further to use the width of the lanes farthest from the center of the pool. The variations in pool and lane dimensions is a small but real factor on performance and future pools will include features most likely to lead to fast times.

BEYOND THE OLYMPICS ... ENDURANCE SWIMMING

What's more impressive is how attention to detail on equipment makes what might appear out of the realm of possibility a reasonable proposition. Diana Nyad is an elite swimmer holding a number of long distance swimming records. She decided to attempt to swim 180 km from Cuba to Key West in 1978. She had to perform the swim while inside a shark tank, which made the journey particularly arduous. She was blown off course and no more than two thirds of the way into her journey and had to quit. She wanted another crack at completing the swim and as she approached her 60th birthday, set that as her goal.

KEY WEST, Florida: Diana Nyad steps onto Smathers Beach in Key West on September 2, 2013, becoming the first person to swim from Havana, Cuba to Key West, Fl. without a shark cage. *Credit: Shutterstock*

Nyad made four separate attempts between 2010 and 2013, tweaking her plan after each failed attempt. She used the equivalent of an electronic shark repellent system, a marker that moved in the water at a controlled rate and in the direction she wanted to swim, and enacted schemes to fuel her and provide rest during the endurance event. The largest issue she encountered was actually jellyfish. During Nyad's first three re-attempts, strong currents pushed her off course and that made the swim longer. She was rather unprotected, swimming in her regular swimsuit, and suffered painful stings from jellyfish and challenges to keep her core temperature up in the open water. Even with those challenges, she got closer and closer to completing her mission with each subsequent attempt.

Her fourth try ended up being successful. Nyad used a silicone face mask, a full body suit, and swam in gloves and booties. There's no question she benefited from the suit, which helped stabilize her core temperature, and may have helped her in terms of swim protection from the jellies and maybe even some added buoyancy [8]. Nyad completed the Cuba to Key West venture in 53 hours, corresponding to an effective swim velocity of ~0.9 m/s—a pretty awesome accomplishment. Interestingly, even today, the marathon swimmer's database still has yet to ratify her accomplishment of the Cuba to Florida swim [9]. It's worth a celebratory mojito either way.

Purists can say what they want with this endeavor, but as far as these authors are concerned, this was a pretty awesome experience and a Cuba to Florida swim probably isn't possible without some level of technical support. Perhaps the best way forward in valuing accomplishment is to give everyone access to the same tools and see who ultimately performs best.

SOFT RIMS

Helping the Shooter's Touch

Basketball is a fast-paced high-scoring team sport and the highest level of competition exists in the National Basketball Association. Teams play five aside and every position has the ability and the need to score the basketball. Scoring is achieved several different ways, but typically through layups, dunks, hook shots, and jump shots. The physics of a basketball shot has been well studied and focuses on factors like launch angle and launch speed of the shot. Less often considered, but important, are the physical properties of the basketball goal itself—the backboard and rim.

THE PHYSICS OF A BASKETBALL SHOT

The launch angle is the angle of trajectory upon release from the player's hands. Launch speed is the velocity (v, figure 1) at which the basketball is traveling upon release and is related to the force at which the player shoots the ball. Launch angle typically decreases the further you are from the rim, while Launch speed increases for longer-ranged shot attempts. In one study, the average two-point shot required a launch speed of approximately 10 miles per hour, whereas the average three-point attempt required 18mph of velocity [1].

The launch angle depends on the shooter, vertical jump, and their defender's height. Shorter players put a larger arc on their shots to prevent defenders from blocking them. A high arc on an attempt creates a larger target for the ball as it approaches the rim, but it is more difficult to control. Gravity will cause increased ball speed. A faster approach velocity means any collision with the rim will increase the bounce from impact and lower success. The slower the ball at impact, the higher the chance that the ball remains close to the impact site, and for a highly accurate shooter, this increases the chances of a successful basket. A successful basket after ricochet is often referred to as a "shooter's touch." [2] Launch angle and velocity are player controlled parameters, but the rim itself plays a critical role in successful scoring.

SOFT RIMS AND STANDARDS

Basketball rims that are more forgiving after imperfect shots are often called "soft" and soft rims are thought to be friendlier to shooters. Soft rims yield shallow rebounds, allowing the ball to bounce around closer to the rim and even carom into a successful basket. Bret Strelow of the *Winston-Salem Journal* investigated the existence of soft rims in a March 3, 2017 article [3]. In the article, Strelow cited examples from ACC NCAA basketball games—a Kennedy Meeks' free throw that took a full lap around the rim before glancing off the backboard and dropping through the net in a North Carolina home win over Louisville, and a Virginia vs. Virginia Tech overtime game where Virginia guard London Perrantes saw a potential tie-breaking layup bank off the backboard, hit the front of the rim, ricochet off the right side of the rim, and bounce off the back plate at least six times before coming to rest on it—which counts as an unsuccessful attempt.

Players have cited soft rims at North Carolina's Dean Smith Center and Duke's Cameron Indoor Stadium as giving friendly rolls. Some regular-season NCAA tournaments have also gained reputations for shooter-friendly rims, such as the Maui Invitational [4]. Some players, so believing in soft rims and their aid to shooters, have admitted to asking teammates to hang on the rim before and during games to soften them.

As far as basketball goal construction is considered, baskets have the rim, the goal or backboard, and the hinges that connect the rim to the goal. The average outdoor playground goal is attached to the ground by a steel pole, while arena or gymnasium goals are commonly suspended from the ceiling rafters and bolted for structural stability. Rims are 18 inches wide on the inside diameter and made from five-eighths-inch rod stock of high strength low carbon steel alloy. Backboards are made from acrylic, polycarbonate, fiberglass, or other metals but the professional ones are more likely a standard composition. In professional competition, the seating requires that the backboard be transparent. Sections 10-12 of the NCAA rules on basketball related to backboards, and the rules describe markings on the backboard, size, and that they should be not tinted, and what they describe as a" transparent, unaltered, rigid rectangular board with a flat surface"[9]. The NBA has had a long term agreement and association with Spalding Corporation as the sole supplier of backboards so those should be standard, whatever they are ultimately made from[10].

Assuming materials are constant, the softness of a rim and its variability can be attributed to how firmly the rim is secured to the backboard. The tightness of the rim can have dramatic effects on the rim's interaction with the basketball and this can be quantified by rebound elasticity (how much a basketball bounces off the rim) and measured using energy absorption (how much of the ball's energy the rim retains after an interaction). To maintain standards for regulated competitions, energy absorption is regularly measured for every rim used in the NBA and NCAA. Section 15, Article 4 of the NCAA rulebook states, "All competitive rings shall be tested for rebound elasticity once before the season (July 15-Oct. 15) and once before the postseason. The rebound elasticity requirement shall be 35% to 50% energy absorption and be within a 5% differential between baskets on the same court."[5] The higher the percentage the, softer the rim and the more forgiving to the shooter. How is this measured? And do soft rims make a difference in the game?

With two tests of the rims required, one wonders whether rims are ever tweaked once measurements are taken. It would be interesting to know what the rebound elasticity is in arenas after a season begins and right before the postseason. It's one thing to readjust rims to be in compliance, it's quite another to gauge the amount of drift over the season, particularly if giants are periodically hanging on the rims.

Determining whether a facility meets standards involves clamping a telescoping rod to the front of each rim and dropping a cylindrical weight (equal to that of a basketball) from a designated height on the rod to a spring-loaded stopping point. A sensor computes the rim's rebound response, and an average score over repeated drops provides the rim's energy absorption. Strelow used energy absorption measurements from eight of the 15 ACC schools and found each to be within the NCAA standards (35-50% and less than 5% difference between opposing baskets on the same count), but ranged considerably within this standard.

Pittsburgh (37.9), Miami (38.3), Clemson (42), and Georgia Tech (44) had the lowest numbers or hardest rims, while the softest rims belonged to Duke (49), Notre Dame (49), North Carolina (48.1), and NC State (45.5). If we look at the difference between home and away True Shooting Percentage (which combines field goals and free throws) for each team, those with with softer rims tended to have a larger difference, or a more favorable shooting percentage at home (Table 1).

These results validate the common thought that softer rims are easier for shooters to score on and produce a higher shooting percentage. While the dataset is small, there seems to be some merit to rim tightness affecting scoring in the NCAA. Softer rims [6] have played a role in the NBA as well, but the NBA has a lower standard range of 20-30% for energy absorption [7] , potentially making it more difficult for shooters in the NBA vs the NCAA.

Team	Home Rim Energy Absorption (Average)	True Shooting Percentage (Home - Away)
Duke	49	8.50%
Notre Dame	49	6.80%
North Carolina	48.1	10.10%
NC State	45.5	15.80%
Georgia Tech	44	1.70%
Clemson	42	2.40%
Miami	38.3	-2.70%
Pittsburgh	37.9	2.60%

CHOCOLATE THUNDER AND THE BREAKAWAY RIM

The NBA's focus on rim tightness began in the 1970s and was centered around player safety [8] when players like the Philadelphia 76ers' 6-11, 250-pound center Darryl Dawkins (aka Chocolate Thunder) began shattering backboards with his thunderous dunks. With his powerful dunks, Dawkins shattered two backboards over a span of 22 days during the 1979-80 season. Showers of glass and a free rim weren't good for player safety and delays required for the subsequent cleanups and repairs to the rim weren't good for the image of the NBA. A new invention helped—the breakaway basketball rim. The breakaway rim has a hinge and a spring where the rim attaches to the backboard that can tilt downwards when pulled on and snap back into horizontal position when released. This allows the rim to flex, then restore itself. This invention revolutionized basketball and allowed the slam dunk to evolve, forever changing the game. Breakaway rims are more forgiving overall—from a dunk or a long range shot—and as can be expected, they have a higher energy absorption than traditional rims.

In 2009, when the NBA introduced a new Spalding Arena Pro 180 goal rim—one that breaks away at the front and sides— scoring in the NBA saw an uptick. Just a week into the season, league scoring averages climbed from 95.2 to 100.0 points per game, field-goal percentage rose from 44.3% to 45.5%, three-point percentage from 33.4% to 36.3%, and free-throw shooting rose from 74.7% to 76.0% when compared to the prior season [6]. These averages regressed over the course of the season but the initial uptick was substantial. The Spalding Arena Pro 180 Goal remains the official rim used in the NBA.

Basketball has evolved tremendously since its early days of peach baskets, and there's no doubt the evolution of the game has been greatly influenced by the interaction of the players and the goals. As outside shooting and the three-point shot have become more prominent in basketball, rims have an even bigger role in the game.

A GENTLEMAN'S GAME

Fans at the Ryder Cup

Patrons for the US and European sides wait for golf action. *Credit: Shutterstock*

U nited States golfers and their fans have the luxury of experiencing two separate but similar biennial international events: the Ryder Cup and the President's Cup. The Ryder Cup is played between U.S. and European golfers on even years, while the President's Cup pits the U.S. against an international team (minus Europe) in odd years. It's an honor to be selected to participate on behalf of your country in either tournament, but perhaps more so for the Ryder Cup, given its long history (the Ryder Cup began in 1927 versus the President's Cup which started in 1994).

These two tournaments are unique from most other PGA golf competitions in that they are national team-based events and their crowds differ greatly from usual, reserved, bipartisan spectators.

THE HISTORY OF THE RYDER CUP AND PRESIDENT'S CUP

The Ryder Cup was named after Samuel Ryder—a British amateur player who donated the original silver trophy. The President's Cup was created by the PGA in 1994 and named after its chairpersons. Each President's Cup tournament has an honorary chairman, the first being 38th U.S. President Gerald Ford. Subsequent chairmen have consisted of prime ministers and presidents, the latest being U.S. President Donald Trump in 2017. Of note, these two tournaments consist exclusively of male golfers. There's a women's tournament equivalent featuring golfers from the U.S. and the Europe called the Solheim Cup, which is played on even years similar to the Ryder Cup.

These tournaments are three to four day events featuring a combination of formats including foursomes, fourballs (best ball), and singles matches. Winners are determined by highest cumulative team score. Unlike other professional tournaments, players aren't paid to participate. Host duties alternate between U.S. and international sites for both the Ryder and President's Cups.

Through 2018, U.S. teams have dominated the President's Cup (10-1-1) and the Solheim Cup (10-5), and ruled the Ryder Cup for much of the 20th century, winning 18 out of 22 competitions. That has changed with the inclusion of continental European golfers in 1979. Prior to the change, U.S. opponents in the Ryder Cup consisted of players from Great Britain and Ireland. Following 1979, players from Belgium, Denmark, France, Germany, Italy, Sweden, and Spain were included. Since the change, the European team has been very competitive.

From 1979 through 2018, the Europeans won 12 of the 20 Ryder

Cups with one tie. Opening up the field of opponents definitely improved the overall skill of the European team, but there are more factors to Ryder Cup outcomes to take into account: nationality and the fans.

HOME COURSE ADVANTAGE AND THE RYDER CUP

Both the U.S. and the European teams consist of top world-class golfers year after year. As a team, the Europeans aren't better ranked than the international competition the U.S. faces in the President's Cup. In fact, the U.S. team often leads by world ranking when compared to Ryder Cup opponents.

Yet, the U.S. dominates its President's Cup opponents and struggles in the Ryder. Looking closer it seems there's some element of home field advantage. Since 1979, the European team is 11-8-1 against the U.S., but over this time the home squad is even better at 14-5-1. The European team has been particularly dominant at home: the U.S. last won the tournament outside its home country in 1993 (over 25 years ago).

The U.S. is 6-4 at home but 2-7-1 away. Paul Azinger, captain of the U.S.-winning 2008 Ryder Cup team, explains that unlike the President's Cup, the European opponent has an advantage of small group bonding which the U.S. doesn't possess[1]. Azinger explains that the International team in the President's Cup doesn't have the same ability to pair like nationalities that the European team does. The pressure to win is also higher at the Ryder, but there are built-in advantages of hosting, such as familiarity of the course, and the large, boisterous, patriotic crowds.

The host venue for the Ryder Cup switches each tournament between the U.S. and the Europe. Within the U.S., host sites have rotated to courses that have hosted the U.S. Open and PGA Championships, which often include stadium-like seating to accommodate large crowds. Increasingly, European Ryder Cup venues have been outside the UK, with the 2018 tournament played at a course called Le

Albratross at a venue called Le Golf in France. The 2022 European Ryder Cup venue is in Italy.

The USGA has assigned host clubs for venues through 2032, including Whistling Straits in Wisconsin, Bethpage Black on Long Island, Hazeltine in Minnesota and Olympic Club in San Francisco. In contrast, the Europeans have chosen home courses that are sites for European Tour Championships but not necessarily in the British Open rotation, including Gleneagles in Scotland, which hosted the Johnny Walker Championship for 15 years, and Valderrama in Spain which was the site of the Volvo Masters.

Just three weeks before the Open Championship held in 2018 at Carnoustie in Scotland, there was a European Tour event at Le Golf in France. A grand total of one likely US Ryder Cup player (Justin Thomas) made an effort to get over to the course and try it out under tournament conditions. Chances are higher that European players have played these courses more than a few times and that U.S. players have likely never seen them [2].

There are different formats for play between best ball, four ball, and singles events. *Credit: Shutterstock*

TOXIC FANS MAKE TOXIC ENVIRONMENTS

In its infancy, Ryder and President's Cup competitions looked not much different than a regular Tour match—far from the aggressive and often toxic environments the tournament can generate today [3]. Some believe the fierce partisanship started in 1985 after a missed putt by the U.S. caused a misinterpreted or inappropriate cheer from the home European team [4]. Respectful golf crowds generally groan at missed putts, cheer when it goes in, and otherwise calm down between shots to a point that professional golfers play in an arena in which quiet signs abound and you can hear a pin drop while a player prepares for his or her shot. Cheering for a missed putt is rare and considered poor-form in golf etiquette.

Nationalism and continentalism has grown at the Ryder, creating partisan crowds [5]. Sentiment is clearly moving away from universal respect for all players. In 1999 at the Ryder Cup in Brookline, Mass-achusetts, U.S. players and fans created a wild and intemperate environment for the visiting European team to the point where Colin Montgomerie's 70-year-old father felt compelled to leave the course, distressed by abusive comments directed by spectators towards his son [4]. Former European team member Howard Clark believes "In the 10 years between 1985 and 1995, the atmosphere changed totally".

The home crowd now relishes the thought of giving an opponent the yips, stabbing at that two-footer to run it by the cup. They border on intimidation, anything for an advantage. Clark notes the catcalling changed his mental approach to the game, affecting his play.

This kind of partisanship is so rare for golfers that it creates a different kind of pressure. Colin Montgomerie was a good player who took more than his brunt of criticism at the hands of U.S.-based hecklers. Montgomerie was heckled so badly at the 1999 Ryder that, in addition to his father leaving on the final day of competition, his U.S. opponent in singles (Payne Stewart) conceded his match early rather than risk further taunts, knowing the Cup had already been won by the Americans. European team member Marc Leishman's wife, Audrey, noted racist, sexist, and threatening comments which don't belong in what has long been known as a gentleman's sport [6]. There are plenty of U.S. players who haven't found the European crowds particularly supportive, either. Some of the top U.S. players have underperformed relative to their rankings and the team format seems to lead to some unnatural pairings that haven't fared well.

The current playing environment is so different from all other professional golf outings that it likely affects who gets selected for the Ryder Cup teams. A number of selections for each team are based on prior performance and typically 2/3 of each team is selected based on a points system that rewards players who have performed better in recent history. The discretionary picks are up to the leadership team for each side, usually in consultation with the players who have already qualified.

Past experience in Ryder and President's Cup competitions can add to the seasoning of the team. Grit and determination and less fragile egos will probably also carry the day for the captain's picks, since they have been battle tested. Captains also look for players who tend to enjoy the format. On the European side, Juan Miguel Jimenez, who was a fixture in the 2000s teams, was battle-tested—quick with the cigars and a smile. For the U.S., Patrick Reed not only relishes the competition but has basked in the partisan crowds—both the glory of the U.S. crowds and neutralizing the rowdy European crowds when away.

CHANGING THE GAME

The Ryder Cup has been a great success in part due to these partisan crowds. In 2016, during a practice round where a U.S. fan heckled European team members struggling with a putt, European golfer Henrik Stenson called out the unruly U.S. partisan patron and challenged him to make a putt of his own [7]. The heckler, David Johnson, sunk the 10-foot putt and got congratulatory celebrations from the players all around.

It was a great moment in the tournament where everyone acknowledged the situation with unruly fans and players had some fun with it.

The European golfers orchestrated the scene well and earned the respect of Johnson and countless other fans for being good sports in a friendly competition. U.S. golfer Justin Rose, who bet $100 on the shot, said it perfectly, "It's fun. We are doing what we should be doing out here—having fun. We are preparing, we are focusing but you have to enjoy it."

Players seem more comfortable playing on the other team's turf. European players now play a larger number of U.S. non-major PGA tour events. Several U.S.-based events including the World Golf Classics are officially European Tour events in addition to the U.S. and PGA Opens held in the States.

Household names like Ian Poulter, Henrik Stenson, Paul Casey, Nick Faldo and others on the European Tour and players from Canada, South America, Africa and Asia have used sponsor exemptions to play more events in the U.S.. A handful of American players have played an extended docket of European tour events, including Mark Calcavecchia and Phil Mickelson. Being better known in the host country and more familiar with the course will likely increase the odds of success.

It's safe to say that there's likely a home field advantage baked into Ryder Cup competition: from the site selection designed to match the features of play of the players chosen as captains to the rowdy home fans. The more these competitions evolve, the better it is for the sport, and as international players become better known, fans and golfers could shift the non-traditional environment of the Ryder Cup from intimating to playful atmospheres. This healthy transformation would hold promise for a more enjoyable event for everyone involved.

SKYBOXES, CROWD NOISE, AND FAN INTERACTION IN THE FUTURE

The view from one of the skyboxes at AT&T Stadium
(home of the Dallas Cowboys), Arlington, Texas.
Credit: Shutterstock

F ans and professional athletes forget that professional sports are businesses. To the fans chagrin, decisions made by upper management and ownership often are bottom line first and winning second. There was a time not so long ago that gate receipts were the biggest reasons teams found themselves in the black or red.

Long before cable TV and sports networks came along to broadcast nearly every game, the bulk of revenue generated from professional sports teams came from gate revenue, parking, concessions, and merchandising. The current major professional sports markets in the United States generated the most revenue from television contracts, league marketing, and overall branding efforts. The sports world is approaching a point where ticket sales are less important to financial success.

TELEVISION CONTRACTS DRIVE REVENUE

There's a growing sense that ticket costs ebb and flow with no relationship to actual supply and demand. Put a better team on the field and it might lead to more ticket sales and might not—it's almost inelastic. Fifty years ago, two baseball teams had their own TV networks. All Chicago Cubs games were on WGN channel 9, in part because the Tribune Company (owners of WGN and the Cubs buying the team from Phil Wrigley of gum fame in 1981), thought it was pretty good content and leveraged their assets. The Atlanta Braves played their games on WTCJ in Atlanta—the genesis of the Turner Broadcasting System—owned by Ted Turner, who also owned the Braves. Turner's ability to put the Braves in front of every cable customer in the U.S. and the Tribune Company's ability to showcase the Cubs nationwide led to a revolution in cable access in sports and ever-increasing network deals for professional and college sports.

Now, professional leagues and the NCAA have TV contracts with content providers, including ESPN, Fox, and self-developed cable networks like the Big Ten Network, Raycom Sports, etc. Broadcast rights are a revenue stream that wasn't conceived of 40 years ago. Now the value of broadcast rights have eclipsed gate receipts (if you discount the value of concessions) as shown by the Price Waterhouse rendering, published in 2017 (Figure 1).

Revenue type / Billions	2012	2013	2014	2015	2016	2017	2018	2019	2020	2021
Media Rights	$ 11.62	$ 12.26	$ 14.59	$ 16.31	$ 18.37	$ 19.07	$ 20.14	$ 20.96	$ 21.76	$ 22.67
Gate Receipts	$ 15.82	$ 17.14	$ 17.44	$ 17.96	$ 18.65	$ 19.16	$ 19.55	$ 20	$ 20.47	$ 20.92
Sponsorship	$ 13.26	$ 13.90	$ 14.68	$ 16.30	$ 16.30	$ 16.66	$ 17.61	$ 18.39	$ 19.34	$ 19.87
Merchandising/Branding	$ 12.77	$ 13.14	$ 13.49	$ 13.81	$ 13.97	$ 14.39	$ 14.55	$ 14.73	$ 14.94	$ 15.09

Financial impact in professional hockey, baseball, basketball and football leagues in the North America, assessed and estimated between 2012 and 2021 (Price Waterhouse) [1]

As a player, you have competing self-interests. On one level, professional athletes and collegians want more goodies—whether pay, media exposure that leads to increased personal marketability, a better weight room, food, accommodations, etc. These same athletes are more likely interested in playing for a crowd and developing their own brand, whether it's on Twitter, Facebook, Instagram, or whatever new medium displaces these. Living and playing in marquis cities (L.A., N.Y., Chicago) costs more to live for these players but, let's face it, the skyrocketing contracts in most of these leagues means none of them are hurting, and the personal brand of these players develops in NYC more than if they are in Oklahoma City or New Orleans. Though as the world becomes more electronically interconnected, the gaps between traditionally large market and small market teams is decreasing but still VERY stark.

WEALTH OF THE NATIONAL BASKETBALL ASSOCIATION

Let's look at the relative value of each organization in the NBA [2]. The thirty teams that comprise the NBA are distributed across the country and there is a wide range of intrinsic values amongst team (see the wealth bar chart shown in Figure 2.) In the figure, the term "sport" constitutes the relative contribution attributed to each team playing games—whether on its home court or visiting others. For this metric, a team that increases sales of other home courts is perceived as more valuable than one that doesn't. Next, is the "market" value, which relates to the intrinsic value of the city and market size in which the team plays. The third element is the home "arena" value which is directly linked to home attendance, luxury box contracts, and other intrinsic uses that can amortize the cost of the arena. The last piece is the "brand" which corresponds to the merchandising potential of the team and its overall marketability. The arena value of the three teams with the largest overall valuations (LA Lakers, NY Knicks, and Chicago Bulls) is more than the TOTAL valuation of the New Orleans Pelicans. If we look at brand variation across the league, linked with the ability to sell the team as a brand for larger merchandising deals, we see there is a pretty large disparity between the NBA haves and have-nots.

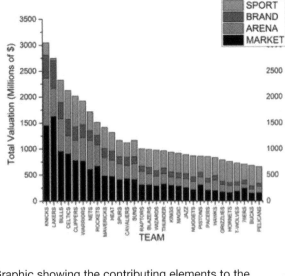

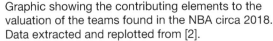

Graphic showing the contributing elements to the valuation of the teams found in the NBA circa 2018. Data extracted and replotted from [2].

In addition to paying players, team owners have to pay facility fees or rent to field the team. Let's take a deeper look at the various NBA basketball venues around the league. Table 1 shows the team, the city, its construction date, any structural renovation date, the relative capacity, the number of skyboxes/luxury suites available, and who actually owns the facility. It's worth noting parity exists between different

basketball arenas. Most NBA arenas can seat 20,000 fans with typically 70-120 luxury suites distributed around the arena. Each box fits
~20 people on average. This means that around 2,000 seats (or roughly
10% of the seats in the stadium) are premium seats.

	Arena	Year Built	Seats	Sky Boxes	Renovation Date	Venue Owner
Warriors	Oracle Arena	1966	19,596	78	1997	Oakland Alameda County Coliseum Authority
Knicks	Madison Square Garden	1968	19,812	89	1991	MSG Company
T-Wolves	Target Center	1990	19,356	68	2004, 2014 & 2017	City of Minneapolis
Jazz	Vivint Smart Home Arena	1991	18,303	56	none	Miller Faily Legacy Trust
Suns	Talking Stick Resort Arena	1992	18,422	94	2003	City of Phoenix
Bulls	United Center	1994	20,917	169	2010	Bulls/Blackhawks
Cavaliers	Quicken Loans Center	1994	20,562	88	2006	Cleveland/Cuyahoga County
Celtics	TD Garden	1995	19,980	90	2007	Delaware North Corp
Blazers	Moda Center	1995	18,624	78	none	Anschutz Entertainment Group
76ers	Wells Fargo Arena	1996	20,328	82	ongoing	Comcast Spectacor
Wizards	Capital One Arena	1997	20,356	110	ongoing	Monumental Sports and Entertainment
Hawks	Philips Arena	1999	18,118	111	2018	City of Atlanta/Fulton County
Nuggets	Pepsi Center	1999	19,155	95	2008	Kroenke Sports and Entertainment
Pacers	Bankers Life Fieldhouse	1999	17,923	71	planning	City of Indianapolis
Heat	American Airlines Arena	1999	19,600	66	ongoing	Miami Dade County
Raptors	Scotiabank Arena	1999	19,800	45	2018	Maple Leaf Sports and Entertainment
Pelicans	Smoothie King Center	1999	16,867	56	planning	State of Louisiana
Clippers	Staples Center	1999	19,060	172	planning	Anschutz Entertainment Group
Lakers	Staples Center	1999	18,997	172	planning	Anschutz Entertainment Group
Mavericks	American Airlines Center	2001	19,200	144	ongoing	City of Dallas
Spurs	AT&T Center	2002	18,418	50	2015	Bexar County
Thunder	Chesepeake Energy Center	2002	18,203	49	2011	City of Oklahoma City
Rockets	Toyota Center	2003	18,055	103	none	Clutch City Sports and Entertainment
Grizzlies	Fedex Forum	2004	18,119	63	2017	City of Memphis
Hornets	Spectrum Center	2005	19,077			City of Charlotte
Magic	Amway Center	2010	18,846	72	none	City of Orlando
Nets	Barclays Center	2012	17,732	101	none	Brooklyn Local Development Corporation
Kings	Golden 1 Center	2016	17,608	34	none	Vivek Ranadive
Pistons	Little Caesars Arena	2017	20,491	62	none	Detroit Downtown Development Authority
Bucks	Wisconsin Sports and Entertainment Center	2018	17,500	34	none	Wisconsin Center District

SKYBOXES HISTORICALLY

The origin of the skybox, or luxury box, has been around since the 1960s. The original Houston Astrodome, built in 1965, contained not only six restaurants, but also a series of luxury boxes catering to corporate sponsors and other rich fans, like team owner Roy Hofheinz who had a complete apartment in the dome [3]. Since the Astrodome was built, most modern stadiums and arenas included these boxes de rigueur.

There is an important distinction between box and non-box seats. Normal gate receipts get filtered through a revenue sharing agreement with the league while luxury box revenues are commonly held by the host/owner. Thus, in new construction, the inclusion of luxury boxes is crucial and historic facilities such as Wrigley Field in Chicago and Fenway Park in Boston have underwent massive renovation plans that have included the carving out of space to dedicate to luxury boxes. Since the seats in these luxury areas are substantially more expensive than upper deck grandstand seats, team owners have been okay with reducing overall capacity to increase the exclusivity of the luxury boxes and tweak the supply relative to a somewhat fixed demand. In the NBA, Madison Square Garden in New York City was built at a time when luxury boxes weren't included in the original design, but subsequent renovations have addressed this potential deficiency. In 2019, when Oracle Arena in Oakland is replaced by an arena in San Francisco, Madison Square Garden will be the oldest NBA arena by more than 20 years.

Oracle Arena is home to the Golden State Warriors, superstar Stephen Curry, and some of the most raucous fans in the NBA. Oracle (nicknamed the Roaracle) is long celebrated as one of the loudest NBA arenas and there's a perceived home arena advantage for the Warriors. During the 2015 playoffs, the eighth-seeded New Orleans Pelicans, without a lot of playoff experience, came out cold against the top-seed Golden State Warriors in the opening game at Oracle. Pelicans players attributed at least some of the cold play to being out of sorts at Oracle with their fans. Pelicans star Anthony Davis mentioned he couldn't hear either his coaches or teammates on the court [4]. Pelicans head coach, Monty Williams, wasn't upset—he was more in awe of what kind of advantage it was for the home team and wished for a similar response in New Orleans. Crowd noise has a clear advantage.

Some teams have tried to increase crowd noise artificially. Marv Albert and Steve Buchantz, announcers for the TNT network and Washington Wizards respectively, both called foul on the Boston Celtics [5] and Miami Heat [6] for amplifying crowd noise and using fake noise during games. Both teams denied any such shenanigans, but it doesn't mean that it couldn't happen. Unlike the NFL, which actually has a rule about fake crowd noise being broadcast over the public address system (violated recently by the Atlanta Falcons [10]), there seem to be no such restrictions in the NBA rule book. There are also rules in the NBA about players not communicating with a player on the free throw line, but not for the rest of the fans in the arena. This sort of fan interactions within the game have been ingrained in the NBA culture (Spike Lee is famously found courtside at Knicks' games often interacting with opposing players during the games [11]).

SKYBOXES AND THE NEW FAN EXPERIENCE

Luxury boxes are equipped with windows that can be shut to block out noise. They have camera feeds through closed circuit TV or a link to the broadcast. The box seats are more plush and roomier than in the actual area. In planning for the future, team owners are in the position where TV camera feed locations have better viewing locations than the actual seats [7]. For an owner interested in making a profit, displacing conventional seating with premium seats has several benefits for the bottom line. It tilts the supply/demand ratio to that of the team owner. It raises the average price of the ticket in the house, and increases exclusivity overall. Luxury boxes are often a way to identify sponsorships and naming rights, often negotiated over a period of years, which makes it easier to predict revenue streams. One bad year of team performance doesn't lead to fewer luxury boxes being rented as it might with single ticket holders.

A view of a luxury suite in AT&T Stadium in Arlington, Texas sight of Packers Steelers Super Bowl XLV. *Credit: Shutterstock*

Maybe in the future, the cost of amortizing a new arena will come not from fans but by thinking of the arena of an anchor of a much larger enterprise. The Golden State Warriors, in the midst of a $1B new arena are looking to amortize the cost through the coordination with other developers to produce high end restaurants, high end condos and business rent, and other schemes to make the arena confines a destination, whether the team is there or not[12]. It doesn't mean that the team owner stops embellishing on what's inside, it's more about co-locating a large number of people who can live and cheer in relatively close proximity to each other. At Golden State, they have ingeniously come up with a monthly ticket option for $100 to co-locate inside the arena but with the stipulation that the ticket neither gives them a seat, nor a view of the game[13]. The option is simply for these "in the house ticket holders" to simply bask in being near the excitement, even if their best view is from a TV monitor near the concessions and bathrooms.

If after the grand arena is constructed and 10% of the crowd is sequestered in these plush sky box rooms, do they cheer and jeer with the same intensity as fans sitting courtside? In this era of Instagram, what fraction of the audience is even following the game? Does any perceived lower intensity in the interest of the fan base actually change how players play defense, go after a rebound, and flop to draw a charge? Is the future a world where fewer regular seats exist and more luxury boxes make the separation between the average fan and the uber rich fan more profound? There will be owners and ownership groups that value the everyday fan, and efforts will continue to make sure warm bodies are in the seats. It's not likely that all seats will be displaced for suites, but there's some cause for alarm if tomorrow's potential fan isn't given the opportunity as a spectator.

There have been sincere efforts to put more fans in seats, and the tactics that might garner the most traction are those focused on recruiting kids—the future fanbase. The Baltimore Orioles, in a rebuilding year, created a promotion in 2018 to give families two free upper deck tickets to every Orioles home game for every adult upper deck ticket purchased [8]. The Kansas City Royals used a promotion allowing fans who enter into a contract to purchase season tickets to actually win them by hitting a home run in batting practice[14].

The legalization of sports betting in US arenas will also play a large role on ticket sales, even if the fans don't purchase the tickets to get a view of the playing surface. It could well be that fans are more attuned to their betting prowess than the actual game itself. Needless to say, while the product on the field has some influence on how many seats and passes are actually sold, teams are using different revenue streams to boost their bottom lines. In the future this could dramatically change the way fans consume games. The traditional route of using promotions like Game of Thrones and Star wars movie nights, bobbleheads, and giveaways may always exist [9], but with real estate, high end retail and restaurants, and legalized sports betting coming to arenas the clientele and associated game climates may be in for an abrupt change.

THE IMPORTANCE OF THE BATTER'S EYE IN BASEBALL

Sections 34 and 35 populated by some Boston fans in 1990. *Credit: Jere Smith*. [4]

The pitcher stands on a mound 60 feet and 6 inches away from the hitter at home plate. When the ball is thrown, from the hitter's perspective, it travels with sections of center field in the background. This is called the batter's eye. With the pitcher standing in an elevated position and throwing overhead, the ball can be framed by seats in center field—occupied or unoccupied—a spectrum of colors and bodies in t-shirts, hats, etc., of different colors. This can interfere with the batter's sight, giving the pitcher an advantage.

It's hard to tell how much of an advantage this can give pitchers, with constantly changing stadium configurations, fan placement, lighting, and color palettes, but the batter's eye has been a topic in MLB circles for years—mainly because of batter safety. It's clearly safer for the batter to at least get a glimpse of a potential beanball and get out of the way, if possible, than have that ball lost in a kaleidoscopic background.

BUILDING A BETTER BATTER'S EYE

By the 1960s MLB owners were encouraged by the league to create center field backdrops in which the color of the seats, walls, and other structures provided a constant contrast to the white ball [1]. For new stadiums in development, like the original Candlestick Park in San Francisco, a square area in center field was designated as non-seating, which affected stadium design and seating capacity. Many stadiums in use long before the 1960s weren't able to create a uniform batter's eye —like where the White Sox, Indians, and Tigers played, along with iconic stadiums like Yankee Stadium, Fenway Park, and Wrigley Field.

Fast forward to today where every ballpark has at least an identified batter's eye region [1]. The exact dimensions of the batter's eye vary at each stadium and these areas are set to contrast the ball and satisfy the spirit of giving the batter a more uncontested look at the ball being thrown to the plate. With the demolition of older stadiums and design of newer ones, the batter's eye issue was solved at these new sites. Only Fenway Park and Wrigley Field remain as legacy parks built before batter's eye concept was instituted.

FENWAY PARK ACCOMMODATIONS

The Boston Red Sox team owners were rather reluctant to discard center field seats in the batter's eye at Fenway Park. At the time, Boston had several left handed pitchers whose pitches were difficult to pick up amongst the myriad of colors of the fans in sections 34 and 35— Fenway's location of the batter's eye. That fact is ironic because the advantage and the health concerns of the batter's eye affect both teams.

In Boston, a local player named Tony Conigliaro was beaned in the face in front of the home crowd in 1967, fracturing his cheekbone, dislocating his jaw, and damaging his retina [2]. Conigliaro mounted a comeback but never really got back to pre-beaning form. Conigliaro's experience made the most compelling reason to block off the seats because he couldn't see pitches very well with so much fan color in the seats. He was the poster child for what could happen. Boston still has seats in the batter's eye, but have made some modifications for batter safety.

The seats in sections 34 and 35 are nearly directly in line with center field. *Credit: Flickr User ChrisDag, Attribution 2.0 Generic (CC BY 2.0)*

Sections 34 and 35 have a black tarp draped over seats to cover them for day games—still allowing seating for night games and other events. The tarp remains off for the duration of the occasional day/night doubleheader for fans that have tickets for both games. Boston, and other teams, have solved this problem by handing out t-shirts the same color as the backdrop for people to wear during the day game portion of the event. By night, the assumption is that lighting is sufficiently dark that people can sit there without substantially affecting the batter's vision.

BOSTON, Massachusetts: Fenway Park on May 23, 2011 in Boston. Fenway Park is one of the oldest professional sports venue in the United States. *Credit: Shutterstock*

MILWAUKEE, Wisconsin: Miller Park, home of the Milwaukee Brewers on July 15, 2009. *Credit: Shutterstock*

STADIUM CHANGES

Some batter's eye areas are simply walled off, painted, tarped off, or landscaped. Detroit's Comerica Park has a fountain in their batter's eye. Even with an appropriately large batter's eye, the decisions of what to put in the center field area can still wreak havoc.

At Target Field in Minnesota, there were 12 dark fir trees that provided dark-green foliage in the batter's eye [1], but apparently, even with the trees, there were fluctuations in color that still made it a challenge to see pitches. They were removed after Minnesota's first season at Target Field and new trees were planted higher up in 2014, not in the field of view of the hitter [5]. In Milwaukee, particularly during day games, there are sky-boxes above the Batter's Eye that catch the sun and reflect a glare that could be worse for the batter than the variable fans' colors. It became necessary to tint the windows in the skyboxes to reduce glare on the field[6]. Improving the view of the batter should reduce the chance that they're more vulnerable to a pitch they don't see [1].

Going back in time, some stadium changes might require a brand new stadium in the long run. Point in fact is Wahconah Park, which has been the home field for a number of minor club teams (A and AA) throughout the 1960s-1980s and most recently is home for the Pittsfield Suns, a collegiate summer league team located in Pittsfield Massachusetts[7]. The park was built in the 1890s and had the misfortune of being situated so that batter at home plate faced directly west. The other field that has this distinction is found in Bakersfield California[8]. This was not much of a problem until 1946 when lights were installed and games started being scheduled later in the day[7]. With the long days of summer, sunsets were occurring directly over the pitcher's shoulder that led to delays of game waiting for to glare to subside. Finally in 1989, a mesh screen was installed in center field to minimize some of the glare which still stands today [8].

Overall, while not complete solutions, changing the area that makes up the batter's eye has improved player safety and neutralized a potential pitching advantage.

UMPIRES AND REFEREES

Influence of Replay on Home Field Advantage

PERPIGNAN, France: Rugby players in action at the
Rugby Top14 French Championship match between
USAP Perpignan and Brive on January 2, 2011.
Credit: Shutterstock

The largest presumed influence that home field advantage has on performance has been the likelihood that there is an effect on the officiating influenced to avoid the wrath of the home crowd. The notion is that a more objective, disinterested third-party might referee the game more accurately and with less bias. Included in the book *Scorecasting* is analysis into how the presence of a large home crowd tends to result in a more favorable strike zone for the home team in baseball, the chance that fewer penalties and fouls are assigned to the home hockey or basketball team, and similar observations[1]. It is logical that the referees, either consciously or unconsciously, are more likely to make judgment calls in favor of the home team simply to avoid being booed out of the arena on any given night. It's not an easy job. The advent and implementation of video replay into American sports has helped take stress off referees and possibly level home field advantages.

HOME FIELD ADVANTAGE

Anyone who has been in a rowdy home environment can feel the influence of the crowd. The relative aid that the jeering fans provide adds to the mystique of certain home venues. Cameron Indoor Arena in Durham, North Carolina is known to be particularly intimidating for opposing NCAA men's basketball teams with its hostile home atmosphere, which likely adds to how many judgment calls are made in Duke's favor. Cameron is not the only stadium with palpable fan influence. Lambeau Field in Green Bay, home of NFL's Packers, is an influential field—especially in games played in the winter months at the outdoor stadium. Major League Baseball's Fenway Park in Boston, home of the Red Sox; Tiger Stadium of the NCAA football LSU Tigers; and Quest Field, home of NFL's Seattle Seahawks are other examples of home fields with presumed influence.

How much of a difference does home field make? In Scorecasting, and prior to video replay, Moskowitz and Wertheim identified the home field winning percentages within different American professional sports leagues as essentially between 50 and 60% [1]. The NBA had the highest home field advantage at 60.5% followed by the NFL (57%), NHL (56%), and Major League Baseball (54%).

THE LINK BETWEEN THE REFEREE AND HOME FIELD ADVANTAGE IS A SHRINKING PROPOSITION.

Referees conferring at the Alabama Football Campingworld Kickoff on September 1st, 2018 in Orlando Florida in a game featuring the Alabama Crimson Tide vs. the Louisville Cardinals. *Credit: Shutterstock*

The issue of instant replay and the capacity of head coaches to ask referees to review their questionable calls through challenges will naturally lead to fewer judgement calls and less of a home field advantage. If there is a particularly egregious play that goes against the home team, a replay will likely show up quickly on the jumbotron, and maybe that helps the coaching staff to decide to throw the challenge flag. One would like to think that everything finds its way to a replay, but if the judgment call goes with the home team and it looks wrong, maybe there is a little less enthusiasm in the replay booth to air that as well. One runs the risk of tripling the time of each game if every play is reviewed [3].

The current arrangement of instant replay in NFL and NCAA football doesn't mean that home field advantage no longer exists, but the prevailing judgment is that home field advantage is of diminishing value. There are still some structural issues relating to the challenge. For example, there are only a limited number of challenges but at the same time, ESPN doesn't have unlimited interest in calling a game with an endless number of challenges. If there is a change of possession, it is compulsory to review those calls and scoring plays are automatically replayed. These are written into the operational rules for the leagues. If a team only gets 2 challenges per game, coaches will typically hold them until it is clear that the referees made a mistake, solely to not lose precious timeouts or the opportunity for future challenges. In tennis, the number of challenges is regulated by the number of sets played. It has been observed that later in a set, players are more likely to ask for a challenge even knowing that is likely to be unsuccessful. It is use-it-or-lose-it with regard to some instances regarding challenging a referee's call.

Player to referee ratios vary by sport. There are seven referees in American football to observe the 22 players on a field. The football field is 53 yards wide and 100 yards long with two 10 yard end zones on each end. The referee team contains a crew chief who lines up behind the quarterback on offense. There are side, field, and back judges to cover the broader field where the offense is played, and two linesman whose primary job is to set the ball on the appropriate field location, and to deal with decisions on measurement by yardstick. That leaves the umpire who is situated near the middle linebacker who is on the front line of the action. The umpire deserves the most hazard pay, particularly for a run oriented offense and where crossing patterns are being executed by the receivers. There are other officiating staff linked with instant replay and resolving challenges but they are not on the field and not making primary calls on the field. The Canadian Football League operates by different rules and their fields are slightly wider, but they have the same general make-up and job descriptions for their seven-member officiating crews. They include a replay official as the eighth referee. In Australian Rules Football, there are also seven judges for a match, although they are called umpires and are distributed differently with obviously different job responsibilities than their football counterparts. There is no in-game replay in Australian Rules Football. In contrast, professional rugby leagues have a video referee but are allowed to make specific on-field judgement calls.

In basketball, there are 15 different types of calls that are reviewed in the NBA through instant replay [8]. They include reviews of calls with little to no time left in a half, flagrant fouls, player altercations, clock malfunctions including resetting the 24 second clock, confirmation of 2-point or a 3-point shot attempts, and goaltending/basket interference claims. Interestingly, the rules also state that a delay of game penalty can be called if a player comes off the bench without having their shirt tucked in, but there are no such calls for players having to retie their shoes on the court. In NCAA basketball, rules about replay usage are slightly more restrictive and include end of time calls, determinations of 2 and 3 point shots, proper assignment of fouls, interpretation calls when players from opposing teams are both involved in pushing a ball out of bounds, and charging/blocking calls late in a game [9]. In tennis and in baseball (MLB), there is a challenge system for calls made allowing review triggered by individual managers and players similar to the NFL [10]. In hockey (NHL), all goals are confirmed by instant replay and there is a central review system for all games [10]. It's safe to say that the current state of major professional sports make some use of instant replay to improve the accuracy of the game.

PHILADELPHIA, Pennsylvania: Two basketball officials watch an instant replay review during an Atlantic 10 basketball conference game on January 19, 2013. *Credit: Shutterstock*

HOW ABOUT PROFESSIONAL SPORTS IN WHICH THERE IS A SMALLER REFEREE/PLAYER RATIO?

We compare the oversight of American football with soccer. Soccer uses three, and at most four, referees with the same number of players as football. Soccer is played on a larger and more distributed field (typical dimensions 65-75 meters wide and 100-110 meters long). There is a head referee and 2 assistant referees on the field. They all have to track the ball. To cover that much field accurately, I suspect soccer referees probably run more than some of the players.

It was only recently that video replay was implemented in professional soccer leagues. Video assistant referees (VAR) were implemented in a 2016 international friendly [4], in Major League Soccer in 2017[5], and the FIFA World Cup in 2018 [6]. The use of VAR is currently limited to goals, penalties, and cards. This has generally been well received as fouls or other faults are occurring away from the ball and behind the referees, there is less chance that the referees in soccer are going to see everything or make the correct call. The continuous clock doesn't lend itself well to large stoppages of play while an individual action is reviewed, so limiting VAR use to plays where there is a natural stoppage is a great introduction of the technology.

Prior to implementation of VAR, soccer had a home field advantage assessed as high as a 69% of winning percentage for home teams [7]. Some of this advantage is apparently due to the general loudness of the crowd and its proximity to the actual field. The referee crew has a much higher potential to impact the outcome of soccer compared to other professional sports like hockey and baseball. It makes sense if we consider that scoring is generally low and how a referee interprets a foul can lead to an expedited chance for scoring, which if successful would have a larger impact in the game compared to higher scoring sports. The handing out of a red card can greatly impact the current game but also determines whether that player can play a subsequent game. If the interpretation of a foul is a judgment call based on the assessment of referees who can be influenced by the home crowd, then these calls are the ones most likely to fall in the favor of the home team. It will be interesting to see if after the implementation of VAR home winning percentages in soccer change.

In the German premier soccer league, an assessment was performed of the relative home field advantage of fields dedicated only to soccer vs more multi-purpose facilities including those that had a running track between the stands and the field. The design was to study fan distance from the field of play. Interestingly, the relative home field advantage shrunk as the distance of the fans to the field increased. It was portrayed that the referees in that league perceived crown noise more directly in more intimate stadiums, then when a 40-50 foot barrier insulated the field from the rest of the stadium [2]. The outcome of this analysis could influence future stadium designs.

In rugby, there are even more players than in soccer, 26 players on a field (13 per team in all), with the match judged by one referee for the game and two "touch judges" and in professional play, a video judge. The referee handles all on the field calls and time stoppages as in soccer, with extra time assigned for no action periods linked with injuries, etc [11]. One would assume a video review would contribute to stoppage time as well.

In the end, referees who judge professional sports are human and not immune to sensing the crowd and the field. They are not always in exactly the right place to see everything and have to make decisions on the field with a limited data set of observations. It is expected that these people are generally unbiased and objective and there exists a perception of unconscious bias that could benefit the home team. This advantage is evidenced by most of the professional leagues having a slight tilt toward the home team winning.

Challenging calls on the field can be increasingly replayed and if some potentially biased calls are undone, the net result is a slightly more competitive and accurate outcome. The most recent additions to replay in professional American sports do not cover all subjective calls, such as an MLB umpire calling balls and strikes differently between the home and away team, but any replay is a start. Raucous places like Cameron Indoor Arena may always be intimidating to opposing players, but the potential influence over the referees may be decreasing.

24

ENDURANCE CYCLING & BLOOD DOPING

HEULGOAT, Brittany, France: Tour de France contestants passing through the village of Huelgoat cheered on by the local people gathered in the main street, on July 12, 2018. *Credit: Shutterstock*

E very July, we're treated to the Tour de France—the most widely known endurance bicycle race in the world. The Tour de France is a multi-stage event where cyclists traverse vineyards, coastal areas, cities, and mountains in and around France. The course changes slightly every year with sprint races, endurance races, mountain stages, and an overall race going at the same time.

Each cyclist faces 21 days of rigorous riding over the span of 23 days—two days for breaks. Each riding day consists of a leg of the race where participants ride more than six continuous hours on their bike. After each leg, riders use the next 18 hours to recover to do it all over again the next day—the pinnacle of athletic endurance.

COL DU GLANDON, France: The peloton riding in a beautiful curve at Col du Glandon in Alps during the stage 19 of Le Tour de France on July 24, 2015.
Credit: Shutterstock

Competitive cycling has been linked with a long standing history of its participants extensively using methods to enhance endurance athletic performance—both legally and illegally—the most notorious of which is blood doping. How prevalent is doping in cycling? One investigation found "65 percent of the riders who finished in the top 10 of the Tour between 1998 and 2013 were either found guilty of doping, or admitted to doping while competing in the event" [2]. Furthermore, "During the time period from 1997 to 2010, 13 out of the 14 winners of the Tour have over time either been found guilty of doping and stripped of their jersey, or have admitted cheating while competing" [2]. These are staggering numbers.

MAXIMIZING ENDURANCE

Endurance athletes will go to great lengths and use many methods to optimize their endurance capacity and elevate their overall competitiveness. The main governing body determining illegal substances in athletic competitions is the World Doping Agency (WADA). The Union Cycliste Internationale (UCI) has incorporated the WADA prohibited list into their own anti-doping rules [7]. The Tour de France is part of the UCI world tour and falls under their guidelines. Substances deemed illegal by the World Anti-doping Agency—those used to gain an endurance edge—include stimulants like amphetamines, blood doping, diuretics, narcotics, and hormones [8]. Here we'll focus on blood doping.

Endurance is regulated by the amount of oxygen conveyed and stored in our bodies. Oxygen is carried and stored in red blood cells (RBCs) within an iron-containing transport protein called hemoglobin. There are three primary ways an elite athlete will try to increase their hemoglobin and thus improve their oxygen capacity: high altitude training, erythropoietin (EPO) injections, and blood transfusions.

| Credit: Pixabay

The amount of hemoglobin and hematocrit are direct measures of blood's oxygen carrying capacity and these can vary with species, age, gender, pregnancy, and resting altitude. High altitude affects more than just humans, and all terrestrial species need schemes to accommodate for the lack of oxygen in the thin air, from mountain goats to the Tibetan sand fox. If an athlete trains at high altitude before performing at a lower altitude, their body will create more hemoglobin to make up for the lower oxygen partial pressures at the high altitude.

Typical hematocrit levels (a ratio of the volume of red blood cells relative to the total volume in a sample of blood) for adult males range between 43-54% of blood volume and for adult females between 38-46%. If an endurance athlete trains at high altitudes long enough to be acclimated, a natural hypoxia develops in their body that naturally raises EPO levels to stimulate production of more red blood cells that carry more oxygen. The stimulation takes time to evolve, so weeks of acclimation are needed. If acclimated in a hypoxic condition, the hematocrit levels can rise as high as 61% in males, and as high as 50% in females [3]. Extra O_2 capacity potentially allows endurance athletes to outperform others who have not acclimated. The general concept of altitude training arose from the Summer Olympics in Mexico City in 1968, a venue with a high altitude (7300 ft, 2.25 kM) [4].

Times in endurance events like middle distance runs and the marathon lagged prior records, but the anaerobic sprinting events saw no such drop-off. Also, most endurance medals were won by athletes from high elevation countries such as Kenya and Ethiopia [4]. As an alternative to high-altitude training, athletes will wear oxygen-depriving air intake masks during training [5] and/or use oxygen deprivation chambers—used primarily while they sleep [9]. Training protocols have been developed to allow athletes to raise their oxygen-carrying capacity through these acclimation pilgrimages. The value of acclimation is temporary as the hematocrit level drops (compensating for breathing more oxygenated air) as someone is re-equilibrated back at lower altitudes,. As the body is limited to the amount of EPO it will secrete, this method of endurance training is generally accepted as legal in competitions.

One can also raise hematocrit by directly injecting EPO at regulated times to recruit more and larger red blood cells, simulating the effect of oxygen deprivation. EPO use is illegal in competitions unless by medical direction. In an open or detectable environment, those injected with EPO will excrete it and its metabolites in their urine at unnaturally high levels. The idea of using EPO for endurance training is based on clinical use with chemotherapy patients. Chemotherapy patients undergo treatments that kill good and bad cells in the body, including RBCs. These patients are often plagued with low hematocrit levels. Injecting these patients with a compound that stimulates increased oxygen carrying capacity compensates for their extreme fatigue during recovery.

The third common way for athletes to increase their oxygen carrying capacity is through blood transfusions. This is also considered illegal in the Tour de France. In this method, the athlete extracts the sera (the non-cellular fraction) of their blood and refills the bloodstream with cellular or whole blood components to raise their hematocrit. This method, while seemingly easier to do, comes with more side effects. Adding back all cellular components increases the number of cells within blood, increases blood viscosity, and raises blood pressures [10]. Larger pressure puts additional strain on the heart to push blood through the body and places the athlete at higher risk of adverse events like blood clots, heart attacks, and stroke [11]. Since 1987, at least 20 European cyclists have died due to abuse of EPO alone [12]. If one is attempting to raise hematocrit levels incrementally, transfusion volumes of a pint or less can achieve the goal. If the blood transfused is from a banked supply from the athlete, risks of infection and transfusion reactions are minimized, though other mortality risks persist.

AVOIDING DETECTION

Elaborate plans have been developed to raise hematocrit through EPO injections by injecting EPO during the off-season to produce hematocrit-rich blood which can be extracted, stored, and transfused into the individual during performance season. The most direct way is to extract a volume of blood from the rider and transfuse them with a volume of erythrocyte- (RBC) rich blood. The goal, under covert operation, is to raise hematocrit levels but not so much as to be detected. Hematocrit level limits are written into the rules of different sports. If only small volumes of the hematocrit-rich blood are swapped, the natural EPO concentration in the injected blood is diluted by the rest of the circulating blood and detection can be avoided.

To learn about the how sophisticated blood doping is, one needs to find individuals who are willing to discuss their training strategies. The goal is to understand the scope of intervention to increase rider competitiveness and that also includes identifying gaps in testing that affect the integrity of cycling. There's plenty of literature on the subject and one report shed light on the annual timeline for an admitted doping cyclist in an article in the British Journal of Pharmacology [6]. The article details how authorities were able to collect rider diaries which showed the depths of covert work to hide the evidence of doping. The off-season (December-February) is the key time to be injected with EPO. By storing blood from these periods, RBC-rich blood was banked for use during the race season, (June and July).

This shows the fairly complicated pattern athletes have used to create maximum performance to avoid detection. This data only speaks to the issues directly relating to blood doping. There have been other schemes to avoid the detection of other banned substances. There are other ways to mask an excessive concentration of EPO in urine, like using diuretics to dilute the liquid evidence. Diuretics trigger renal flushing, inducing urination and thereby diluting the concentration of EPO. As a result, diuretics are also considered *banned substances* at least as far as the Cycling Federations are concerned.

	1	2	3	4	5	6	7	8	9	10	11	12	13	14	15	16	17	18	19	20	21	22	23	24	25	26	27	28	29	30	31
November																				●		●		●		●		●		●	
December																															
January	●		●		●		●		●		●	●																			
February	●		●		●		●		●			●	●	●	●	●	●	●	●		●		●		⊘						
March					●												●														
April												●		●															●		
May								●	●	●	●	●	●	●	●		○		○		○		○		○		○		○		○
June	◉																						◉								
July		●									○									○											
August																															
September																															
October												●		●																	

An example training/doping schedule for an elite cyclist training for bicycle races or events denoted as lines including the Tour de France race in July. The black dots correspond to EPO injections to raise blood hematocrit levels. The open red circles correspond to blood draws and the filled red circles are infusions. The goal is to raise hematocrit without causing a large spike in measured EPO. The months are in the first column and the dates of each month are shown for individual rows for each month. (Data, retabulated from C. Lundby et al, 2012, The evolving science of blood detection, Br.J. Pharmacology,165, 1306-1315).

Endurance cycling is an example of a rigorous athletic event increasingly susceptible to efforts to tweak the participating athlete's performance capabilities. Using blood doping as one example, athletes will go to extremes to manipulate their own physiology to gain a competitive edge. Sadly, the payoffs are enormous—fame, notoriety, and wealth. Those allures can be enough for anyone to take the associated health and public relations risks. Lance Armstrong, once the most celebrated athletes in Tour de France history, is now a symbol for doping. His career completely inverted as he was banned for life and stripped of all of his titles when found guilty of blood doping.

Why are penalties so severe? Penalties imposed by sanctioning agencies are necessary. Studies show when there are no risk of penalty, athletes are more apt to cheat [13]. This leads to a cat-and-mouse game that escalates penalties to a level of banishment from sports all together. The future of endurance events like the Tour de France and the Ironman Triathlon will hinge on rules around what is legal and what's considered an unnatural advantage.

| Credit: Shutterstock

MASCOTS, RALLY MONKEYS, FLORA AND FAUNA, BOTH ALIVE AND DEAD

How Costumes, Animals, and Carcasses Affect the Game

Y ou might discount the potential that non-players could affect games in some distinct way. There are instances, both planned and unplanned, in which the presence of non-human species affect play in some way. These can exist as valuable diversions and part of the goodwill of various sporting ventures or break the tension in a meaningful and competitive game. They can be part of the spirit or branding campaigns to attract fans (like the Rally Monkey for the Los Angeles Angels in 2000), or superstition (like the Chicago Cubs' Curse of the Billy Goat in 1945). Then there are instances where the presence of animals is simply unavoidable. These are the instances we'll focus on here.

ANIMALS TO ENHANCE A TEAM/SPORT BRAND

In tournament events at the professional ranks, there are often charity projects that are endorsed as part of the overall campaigns to recruit fans, raise awareness, and enhance the branding of an event. Typically, golf and tennis tournaments often feature identified charities that are indirectly supported by gates receipts, and there are also often featured events not necessarily part of the graded tournament. The Masters in

Augusta sponsors a par-3 tournament for charity in which families of golfers and other VIPs participate. Do anything at Augusta National and people will come. The US Open in tennis sponsors Arthur Ashe Kids Day featuring celebrities, musical entertainment, and usually some feeble tennis exhibitions from retired players.

For three years running, the International Tennis Foundation (ITF) sponsors a tennis tournament in Sao Paolo, Brazil. Exhibition tennis matches are part of the tournament and, instead of ball boys and ball girls retrieving balls during the match, the staff has trained a number of shelter dogs to perform[1]. The players are happy to play along, as the matches are essentially meaningless and it's all for a good cause, and if the Brazilian equivalent of the Humane Society gets money and some shelter dogs get adopted during the tournament, that's all the better. While the animals are clearly there, the outcomes from these matches are hardly a concern. It's more about the show.

STRIKING FEAR INTO YOUR OPPONENT...MASCOTS!

BOULDER, Colorado: Colorado University, whose teams are called the Buffaloes, eventually may have the biggest mascot on the collegiate scene. A student, Mahlon White of Pueblo, Co., donated this bison calf, who is about half of his full growth, to the University. Left to right: White, Bill McKinney, Rog Hefter, Leonard Weiss, and Warner Bromgard. March 21, 1957. *Credit AP*

Another place where animals might interact in and around the field are as mascots. Most schools adopt a mascot based on some sort of selection process. Often it's based on features and attributes of where the school is situated. Western teams feature broncos, ponies, and other horses. Some areas of the Delaware/Maryland/Virginia coast were a swamp at the beginning of the republic, and the folks from The University of Maryland have named their teams after a type of local turtle. At the University of Florida, they're the Gators. In the Midwest, many of the college teams are named after various wild rodents and weasels, going back centuries in some cases to the heights of fur trapping.

A university, looking to use their mascot to advance their team's performance, is likely to pick something intimidating and menacing. A colleague mentioned that the reason Carnegie Mellon University was no good at sports was because their team mascot was the Tartans, wore woolen fabrics, and the band came out at halftime donning kilts. Braveheart might work in the theaters in surround-sound, but apparently seeing the Tartans on the schedule doesn't cause opponents' hearts to skip a beat. Then again, Stanford's mascot is a tree and they field competitive teams.

If you want your mascot to be intimidating and menacing, it has to be a controlled inspiration. The universities that have done best in satisfying these criteria are the University of Colorado and the University of Texas at Austin[2]. Colorado has had a series of live buffaloes that they run onto the field, all named Ralphie, and when one hears and sees the likes of a prehistoric wooly mammoth running around the field (albeit lassoed by an army of duly decorated animal handlers) it's impressive. Almost as impressive as seeing Bevo, the University of Texas longhorn bull, who also walks the venue for each home football game. Other schools have impressive animal mascots, including Air Force with the peregrine falcon and Auburn University who have multiple mascots and some peculiar linkage to the eagle [2]. Apparently, a wild eagle was observed soaring above the field during a game decades ago and the lore was established. The only issue with these mascots is that in a stadium of 70,000+ people, you need binoculars, or the big screen, to actually see these fearsome mascots.

Other schools have mascots like bears, lions, and tigers, but sadly, they're caged (likely for insurance purposes), like the tiger at Louisiana State University. Teams can also pipe in the sounds of their mascot like the Nittany Lion at Penn State. Increasingly, mascots are caricatures of themselves, like the overgrown-looking turkey called the Hokiebird at Virginia Polytechnic Institute and State University, The Oregon Duck at Oregon, Bucky the Badger at Wisconsin, and Willie the Wildcat at Northwestern. It's a sad sight to see real animals caged on the sidelines.

The HokieBird mascot from Virginia Tech in action on the sidelines. *Credit: Shutterstock*

One year at Northwestern in the 1970s, while Brian lived nearby, the brain trust linked with spirit on the sidelines came up with the slogan "Expect the Unexpected" for the upcoming football campaign and had the grand idea of caging the collegian wearing their Willie the Wildcat outfit— letting the mascot out after each successful scoring drive. Anyone who remembers NU football back then will remember that they were not very competitive, and Willie spent most of the game that year caged, with only a halftime respite for a bathroom break. Willie wasn't NU's first mascot. That honor belonged to Furpaw, a bear cub loaned on Saturdays from the Lincoln Park Zoo, who attended games with handlers during the 1923 season [3]. Furpaw's presence wasn't a good luck charm in 1923, and after that season's losing campaign, his services were no longer required. In 1924, a newspaper describing a game that year helped coin the nickname "Wildcats" when describing the team's tenacity [3].

In the end, if the presence of a mascot triggers good thoughts in the home team, or fear in the brains of the visitors, mission accomplished—however said mascot was deployed.

FLORA AND FIXED OBSTACLES

While trees and flowers are part of the hazard territory in golf, one doesn't expect to have the same types of encounters in other fields of play. But as the story goes, years ago, long before the Braves left Milwaukee for what was then Atlanta Fulton County Stadium, long before Ted Turner bought the Braves and aired their games on WTBS... long before Ted Turner, for that matter (he was born in 1938), there was baseball in Atlanta with a minor league team in Atlanta called the Crackers. The Crackers played their games on a field called Spiller Park which was renamed as Ponce de Leon Park in 1932 for the street the park abutted[15]. Spiller Park was normal in most every way except that the outfield fence did not go from foulpole to foulpole. A patch of grass extended in center field that jutted further out and there was this massive magnolia tree that was in the field of play there. Poncey stadium was the only place where minor league rules had been established as to how to deal with balls that were lost under the magnolia, etc [15]. It was such a beautiful tree that the owners finally finished the outfield wall in 1946 [16] and players hitting the tree were rewarded a home run.

ANIMALS: DEAD

Another way animals have impacted sporting events has been as a disruption. Since 1954, at Detroit Red Wings hockey games, bunches of expired octopi have been hurled from the stands [4, 5]. The tradition dates back to the legacy days when a team only had to win two series to capture the Stanley Cup, Two series, four wins each—that equals eight wins. Eight legs, looks about right. The launching of an octopus onto the ice, with someone having to scrape it up and carry it off, is on par with the general fan interest.

In Detroit, PETA has encouraged the Red Wings to crack down on octopi launchings, and with the move to a new arena in 2017, fans are no longer allowed to throw them onto the ice—but the spirit of the Octopus has been embraced, with two caricature octopus mascots, both named Al, hung from the rafters at the new arena.

With league expansion, other animals have found their way to the ice surface. Copycat launchings of other creatures have included catfish in Nashville [7], the occasional shark in San Jose [8], rubber rats in Florida [9] and a salmon in Vancouver [8]. It's one thing to want to toss a dead animal onto the ice—it's a different thing to get it through security—and a variety of ploys have been used to get this contraband into the arena. How someone could get a four-foot shark through security and toss it onto the ice in San Jose is still a work of genius. Apparently, the shark was strategically strapped to a fan's back, who then wore a large overcoat to hide the evidence.

ANIMALS: GONE

The funniest and best example of how one can leverage home field advantage using prior animals, bar none, is Clark Field, home of the UT Austin baseball team from 1928-1974[15]. Clark Field was unusual in that there was a kind of upper outfield in center field that was 10 meters higher than the rest of the ballpark. Add to it that there was this 30 foot cliff that a batter stared at, and a trail called the Billy goat trail up the left center gap that allowed the center fielder to get from the lower level to the upper level. Wikipedia said that the configuration of the field made the game interesting but we imagine it was a huge advantage to the UT team[16]. Balls caroming off of the cliff went in all directions, teams struggled as to where to place outfielders, and the left fielder was often in the best position to run up the hill to retrieve a ball on the upper deck. It must have been quite a farce to observe the play there. During a stretch from 1949-1974, the longhorns won the national championship twice, finished runner up once, and was in the collegiate world series 12 out of the remaining 23 years[17], that's a pretty good run.

ANIMALS: ALIVE!

Live animals can have a larger impact on the game, and it's important to take into account the size of the playing field relative to the size of animals. There are worms and ants in the average grass playing surface, but they're too small to impact the game in any appreciable way.

There are fields so large that no one can patrol them entirely. Golf courses typically cover a lot of acreage, making it a challenge to eradicate all living animals within its boundaries. Large wire fences surround Augusta National, and it appears that most everything has been driven away, including birds. Maybe gophers sneak in at night, but they wouldn't last long enough to mire the pristine view in April. Elsewhere, shorebirds and other small animals have been observed during golf tournaments, and accommodations need to be made for the errant shore bird who has a well struck golf ball in its beak[12].

The rules suggest that if it's clear that a ball has been moved or removed by an outside agency (see crow, black), no penalty exists and the player is allowed to place a new ball as near to where the agent dislodged the ball from its resting place. Hence, there is no need to retrieve that ball, and with the practically continuous coverage of higher end golf tournaments, it's easier to identify an instance when an animal runs off with a ball and know where to place it.

Some animals have been in the wrong place at the wrong time. Randy Johnson of the Arizona Diamondbacks euthanized a bird with a fastball during a spring training game in 2001[10]. In 2009, at the AT&T Center in San Antonio on Halloween night, San Antonio Spur Manu Ginobli swatted a bat to the court during game[11], triggering a rabies shot, a new nickname (BatManu) and a job offer with Terminix.

One sport where animals have had a profound effect on the event is yachting. It's not possible to clear the water of all living creatures during a yacht race, and in 2005, a South African boat training in the qualification for the America's Cup ran into a whale, completely stopping the boat and seriously injuring two crew members (likely along with the whale as well)[13]. It goes to show that the larger the venue, the more of a challenge it is to liberate it of all living creatures during play.

On a much smaller scale, animals can be a nuisance and affect the players on the field. Progressive Field, the home ballpark of the Cleveland Indians, is very close to Lake Erie, and at certain times of day later in the fall part of the season, flying bugs called midges congregate on the field [14]. Midges look for humidity found on players, particularly pitchers, and there have been instances where midges have swarmed the heads of pitchers at Progressive Field. If a pitcher is going to play for the Indians, it might be good if they prepared themselves and got familiar with these bugs and find a way to not be bothered by them. If the bugs bother a pitcher, chances are the pitcher will work faster on the mound and not be as deliberate as they might be without the bugs around. It pays to find a way to ignore this.

ARRANGING THE FIELD DIFFERENTLY

New Formations, Schemes to Defend, Attack, and Change the Dynamic

In team sports, there are a fixed number of competitors on the field at one time, and their particular positions are usually meaningful. In hockey, goalies are equipped differently than defensemen and wingers and centers. In baseball, we think of batteries (pitchers and catchers), infields, and outfields. In football, we distinguish between offensive and defensive players, and from there, we define distinctions between linemen who block, receivers and backs who catch and run with the ball, and defensive players—linemen, linebackers, defensive backs, and safeties. In soccer, there are all sorts of configurations of 11 players, mainly as a function of the attributes of the team and the knowledge base of the coach.

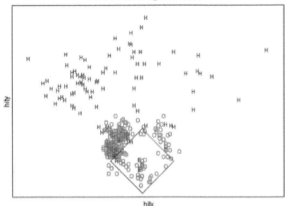

Jose Bautista's groundballs

Jose Bautista's hits (H) vs outs (O) distribution for a given series of at bats, with permission from M. Marchi, baseballprospectus.com.

POSITIONING A SINGLE PLAYER

Rules for how to organize teams in the field of play allow for some flexibility. For single players, the pitcher in baseball is required to have at least one foot adjoining the pitching rubber which is a fixed distance from home plate. The pitching rubber is a plate at least 18 inches long and 4-5 inches wide. Major League Baseball rules don't describe exactly where the pitcher has to have a foot. The pitcher can pitch anywhere from the first base side to the third base side of the rubber, so long as one foot is still attached to the rubber and the pitcher pushes off while throwing to the plate. The catcher has to be behind the plate and not in the path of the baseball bat of the opposing player batting.

In soccer, there's a zone in which the goalie can use his or her hands. Goalies can be situated anywhere on the field, but if they want to use their hands, they need to be located near the goal. To perform a throw in, the throwing player needs to be outside of the playing surface. In basketball, players shooting free throws can be as close as the free throw line but as far back as they'd like.

SWAPPING PLAYERS OR POSITIONING THE FIELD FOR COMPETITIVE ADVANTAGE

In close hockey games, it's not uncommon for the trailing team to yank their goalie and replace them with a sixth skater for the last few minutes. The reward for the sixth skater is that it generates a natural power play opportunity for the team that pulled its goalie. Games in which the goalie is pulled are fast and furious and can sometimes lead to natural advantages leading to a goal to tie the game. The risk in pulling one's goalie is that should the opposing team gain possession of the puck, it's a lot easier to score on an empty net. One wonders whether some team might adopt a hybrid goalie model in which the goalie is less of a goalie and more of a skater. It would wreak havoc on the over/under but might make the game even more exciting.

In basketball, a lot of defensive schemes are five-on-five, man-to-man defenses in which players match up with each other. Some players on offense are more potent playmakers than others who might be on the court for their defensive skills, to rest a more competitive player, or to improve the team's rebounding, for example. The NBA has now been acquiring positional data of 10 dots on a grid over each game now for a number of years, and armed with data, it's possible to tease out the data retrospectively to ask questions about the risk reward scenario linked with double-teaming any one player in general. It's a huge database and it's now in the realm of data analytics to actually probe whether it's worth double-teaming player A and not guarding player E on any one team [6].

In baseball, there are all sorts of crazy schemes to organize the defense to encourage batters to hit into an out. The normal configuration for a defense is symmetric where the battery and the center field are situated on a line bisecting the field, and the left fielder is situated on one side of that line with the third baseman and shortstop and equally opposed by the right fielder and the first and second basemen on the right. For a player who has a more random chance to distribute hits into the playing field, that seems like a pretty good scheme—three in the outfield and four in the infield typically.

In baseball, there are situations when the game is on the line and the winning run is on third base. A defensive team can pull in their infield defenders or stack the infield with an extra player from the outfield to increase the chances that a ground ball put into play will result in an out from the beefed up infield. Put in a pitcher who is more likely to yield ground balls and a team can work their way out of a jam. Desperate times call for desperate measures, and if a ball makes it to the outfield, the run is more likely to score.

This explosion in analytics has meant that increasingly, data is available to suggest how often anyone strikes out, what kind of pitch the like and don't like to swing at, whether they hit a ground ball vs. a line drive, and where they usually put the ball into play. All this metadata can be used in scouting reports, which teams can use to create new types of defensive schemes to put more fielders where the hitter is likely to hit the ball.

Look at what's available. The figure below is the kind of data available on hits, outs and errors on ground balls produced from slugger Jose Bautista [1]. The density of balls hit to the third base side of the diamond make Bautista a better candidate for an infield shift towards third. These kinds of stats are now available for every batter, and the ability to curate big data analytics means that managers can microtarget their defenses, pitcher/batter choices and how to pitch to increase the chances that a batter hits balls to a specific location.

On one end of the spectrum is the notion to change how many outfielders vs. infielders there are. Batters more likely to hit a fly ball might encounter defenses with four outfielders. It was well documented years ago that a little used pinch-hitter and substitute player named Saturnino (Nino) Escalera, who played sparingly in 1954 for Cincinnati (the Red Legs then, now the Reds), was inserted as the first documented effort to create four outfielders and no shortstop. Escelera packed a remarkable series of pioneer experiences into that one season. He was the first black player to integrate the RedLegs earlier in the season and credited as the last left-handed player to play at shortstop in MLB.

Stan Musial was at bat and represented the tying run with one man on and Cincinnati leading 4-2 in the bottom of the ninth against the St.

Louis Cardinals at Busch Stadium. Musial was surprised with the field configuration and complained to the home plate umpire, but as long as there were no more than nine players on the field, all was fine. Maybe Musial was rattled and eventually struck out. The archival box score [2] indicates Escalera as replacing the other shortstop which was true when he was inserted, but Escelera didn't play where the other shortstop had been situated. Escalera was eventually replaced by a third shortstop which was likely after Musial's strike out, but what's ironic is that there was no way to credit him with his unusual position for Musial's at bat.

Box score for the Cincinnati Redlegs vs the St. Louis Cardinals, May 22nd, 1954. *Credit: Baseball-almanac.com*

The unusual configuration of the team was documented by a graphic in the *St. Louis Post Dispatch* as well as by choice comments from manager Birdie Tebbets, who must have been quite a talker. He mentioned that it was the peculiarity of the long straight section of Busch Stadium's right field fence that was also shallow. Tebbets placed the outfielders to optimize how quickly one could return the ball to limit Musial to a single if he hit the wall. Tebbets told a reporter from the Post Dispatch that "Since I couldn't put a player on the roof, I did the next-best thing was adding a fourth outfield to prevent the only other kind of hit that would have bothered me." [2, 3]

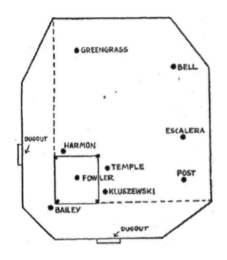

Bird's-eye view of how Cincinnati arranged their defense using a "shortstop" in right field. *Credit: Tom Swope, Sporting News, June 2, 1954.*

DATA ANALYTICS IS INCREASING THE USE OF SHIFTS

The four-member outfield has been used sparingly since the Escalera era, primarily for players who tend to swing for the fences and have more pull on ground balls. Joe Maddon seems to be the largest disciple amongst current managers and he went the distance to install four outfielders and moving the third basemen behind second base for Travis Hafner in recent history. There have also been increasing instances when rather than four conventional outfielders, the second baseman drifts into right center and the other outfielders adjust to the extra coverage. A strongly hit ball to the outfield might still yield a 4-3 ground out with the second baseman playing very deep.

There's a long history in terms of shifting defenders from the natural configuration to match the likelihood balls get hit to one side of the field or another. This notion of shifting the defenders goes back as far as 1877, and sometimes was brought out for specific hitters. Lou Boudreau, player manager for the Cleveland Indians, was looking for a way to neutralize Ted Williams. In the midst of a doubleheader, Boudreau implemented a shift, given that Cleveland had allowed Williams to hit three home runs in game one. These more dramatic shifts were seen as fairly rare, but implemented for a few specific players.

For a dead pull hitter, there are increasingly creative configurations of fielders. Seth Smith of the Padres and Mariners has encountered four infielders between first and second base. The third baseman is supposed to cover anything between second and third, with some help from the fielder standing near second. Defensive strategy for player positioning is also situational. First and third basemen often move a little closer to the foul lines later in a baseball game to accommodate a no doubles defensive strategy. Balls hit down the lines often result in extra base hits, and this is a way of limiting potential damage. With the data, a team manager can now opt to configure the field defense as he or she sees fit.

The Dodgers infield, arranged against Seth Smith on August 29th, 2014 [4]. There are four infielders between first and second and the third baseman near third base.

THESE SHIFTS ALSO OCCUR IN MORE THAN JUST BASEBALL

In football, there are some unusual configurations of offenses and defenses, but there are some additional rules about how players line up. On offense, there are five interior lineman, the tackles, guards, and center that have to line up accordingly and the center usually initiates play by snapping the football to the quarterback. The center does not have to be the snapper, and if a guard or tackle snaps the ball, that is called an unbalanced line. There are other rules about being on or off the line of scrimmage, but at least players are situated on the line of scrimmage for the offense based on rules for the NCAA and NFL. Players on defense can essentially line up wherever they want, usually in the spaces between where offensive linemen line up. One can crowd the line on defense with as many as all 11 players and anyone can rush the quarterback. A team rushes all defensive players at their peril as they would be vulnerable to big pass plays if the opposing quarterback can throw accurately under pressure.

The defense doesn't as have many rules, although no players can line up in the neutral zone—a one-yard region of separation between the offense and defense. So-called goal line defenses can stack the line as many as all 11 players on the defense. Those types of defenses are called to counter obvious running plays. There are plenty of things both offensive and defensive players cannot do that result in infractions penalizing the offending team.

There have been a variety of configurations for both defenses and offenses that can be organized with the notion of a gimmick or a trick play. Some of these configurations are designed to confuse the defense, or to disguise the evolution of a play, while others require position players to be in unusual locations and can be a giveaway of a trick play. A great example is the so-called train or centipede play executed by the University of Michigan football team against Wisconsin in 2016, where the team devolves from the line up below taken in a YouTube video snapshot to this formation just before the snap. It's a simple trick to not give away the formation too early.

In soccer, there are any number of configurations for how the 11 members of a soccer team can be organized on the field. It's generally assumed that everyone needs a goalie. The typical soccer goalie is not weighed down by substantially larger padding and he/she can play upfield away from their goal so long as they function as a non-hands player. Perhaps the most common configuration of the other 10 players on a team is a 4-4-2 arrangement in which there are four defenders, four midfielders, and two offensive players. These distinctions are rather arbitrary as a team moves from defense to offense, midfielders can play offensive roles and even defenders can get into the mix.

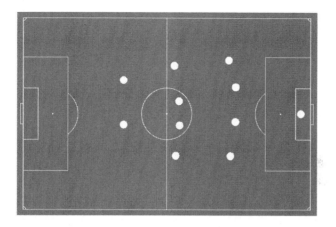

Planning board for plan tactic 4-4-2 in football (soccer) match

Deviations to the 4-4-2 result when coaches ask for more offense from the midfielders or fractionate the fours into smaller increments. From the viewer's perspective, the boundaries between defenders and midfielders seem rather fluid, as when on defense the goal is to get the ball back, and up-fielders drift back to help. A recent article mentioned seven crazy configurations in soccer and who employs them [5].

The average soccer player, who plays a 90-minute match, must expend a lot of energy and only a few substitutions are allowed. FIFA, the body that coordinates the World Cup, only allows three substitutions to occur over the entire match. It could be that these substitutions coincide with a change in the organization of the team configuration to leverage a fresh offensive player who was installed vs. the rest of the defense who might be more gassed. The impact of these differences in how the team is constructed should not be discounted, but from a spectator's vantage point, the difference between a 2-2-2-2-2 arrangement and a 4-4-2 arrangement might not look particularly different. All players are moving around which blurs the boundaries.

There are key times when the dynamics of swapping personnel, or moving around the defensive alignment, leads to a better outcome for a team. If history has any basis, putting defenders where hitters are more likely to hit a ball leads to a better chance to field or catch a ball. If the player executes in a more optimum location, the likely outcome for the team is also better. There are instances where other team configurations are presented mainly as a diversion to avoid larger amounts of defense or offense reading before play is initiated.

ENDNOTES

CHAPTER 1.

1. MLB. *Official Baseball Rules*. 2018; Available from [http://mlb.mlb.com/documents/0/8/0/268272080/2018_Official_Baseball_Rules.pdf].
2. Pashman, A. *Tampa Bay Rays: Installing New Turf at Tropicana Field*. February 8th, 2017; Available from [https://rayscoloredglasses.com/2017/02/08/tampa-bay-rays-new-turf/].
3. Dragoo, J.L., H.J. Braun, J.L. Durham, M.R. Chen, and A.H. Harris, *Incidence and risk factors for injuries to the anterior cruciate ligament in National Collegiate Athletic Association football: data from the 2004-2005 through 2008-2009 National Collegiate Athletic Association Injury Surveillance System*. American Journal of Sports Medicine, 2012. 40: p. 990-995.
4. Bowen, J. *Ethics Amidst the Quirks & Culture of Baseball: A Response to Jack Bowen's Grass-Cutting Concerns*. 2014 May 14, 2014; Available from [http://law.scu.edu/sports-

law/ethics-amidst-the-quirks-culture-of-baseball-a-response-to-jack-bowens-grass-cutting-concerns/].

5. Moskowitz, T.J. and L.J. Wertheim, *Scorecasting*. 2011, New York: Crown Publishing

6. Bois, J. *Home Advantage In Sports: A Scientific Study Of How Much It Affects Winning*. SBNation.com 2011 January 19, 2011]; Available from [https://www.sbnation.com/2011/1/19/1940438/home-field-advantage-sports-stats-data].

7. Cantania, J. *Is Home-Field Advantage as Important in Baseball as Other Major League Sports?* October 9th 2013; Available from [Is Home-Field Advantage as Important in Baseball as Other Major League Sports?].

8. Zumsteg, D., *The cheater's guide to baseball*. 2007, NYC: Houghton Mifflin Publishing

9. Sigal, C. *It's not cheating if you're not caught*. April 7th, 2007; Available from [https://www.baltimoresun.com/news/bs-xpm-2007-04-08-0704060286-story.html].

10. Dickson, P., *The Hidden Language of Baseball: how signs and sign stealing have influenced the course of our national pastime*. 2009: Bloomsbury Publishing

11. Smth, G. *Grass Always Looks Greener Now on the Padres Home Turf*. April 13th, 1987; Available from [http://articles.latimes.com/1987-04-13/news/vw-474_1_home-field].

12. *Harold Bossard, former stadium groundskeeper*. May 2nd, 1994; Available from *Elyria Chronicle Telegram* (Elyria, OH).

13. Sweeney, A. *Ex-Sox Groundskeeper Bossard dead at age 80* February 1st, 1998; Available from [https://www.chicagotribune.com/news/ct-xpm-1998-02-01-9802010313-story.html].

14. Smith, G. *Diamond Cutters*. September 21st, 1998; Available from

[https://www.si.com/vault/1998/09/21/249183/diamond
-cutters-the-bossards-baseballs-first-family-of-
groundskeeping-have-been-perfecting-the-tricks-of-their-
trade-for-three-generations-creating-fields-that-give-the-
home-team-an-edge].

15. Greenville.com, *Roger Bossard Constructing Field at New
Downtown Stadium* 2018. www.
greenville.com/news/drive1205.html

16. Wikipedia. *Roger Bossard*. 2018; Available from
[https://en.wikipedia.org/wiki/Roger_Bossard - cite_note-
autogenerated1-2].

17. UPI(UnitedPressInternational), *Cubs foes look down on
new issue--height of infield grass*, May 29th, 1985, LA
Times, http://articles.latimes.com/1986-05-18/sports/sp-
21214_1_cubs-manager-jim-frey

18. UPI(UnitedPressInternational), *Grass is lean and Cubs
mean with Dunston at shortstop*, May 18th, 1986, Orlando
Sentinel, http://articles.orlandosentinel.com/1985-05-
29/sports/0300250144_1_wrigley-field-grass-cubs

19. Ortiz-Healy, V., *The ivy and the infield: what it takes to
keep Wrigley Field beautiful*, October 4th 2016, Chicago
Tribune,
http://www.chicagotribune.com/sports/baseball/cubs/ct-
wrigley-field-grounds-maintenance-met-20161004-
story.html

20. ESPN, Philadelphia Phillies Pitching Statistics, 2018,
http://www.espn.com/mlb/team/stats/pitching/_/name/phi

21. Gelb, M., *New grass should help Phillies infielders*, April
9th, 2016, Philadelphia Inquirer,
http://www.philly.com/philly/sports/20160410_New_gra
ss_should_help_Phillies_infielders.html.

22. Future Sox Draft Tracker, 2016,
http://www.chicagonow.com/future-sox/2016/06/2016-
futuresox-draft-tracker/

23. O'Connell, P.M., *How Soldier Field's switch from Illinois*

to New Jersey sod caused complaints about turf conditions to nearly disappear, Chicago Tribune, November 22nd, 2018, https://www.chicagotribune.com/news.ct-met-soldier-field-grass-turf-20181120-story.html

24. Rapanich, J., *The world's 18 strangest stadiums*, Popular Mechanics, May 12th, 2010, https://www.popularmechanics.com/technology/design/g279/worlds-strangest-stadiums-gallery/?slide=17

25. Birkett, D., *Detroit Lions players blast 'awful' Arizona Cardinals field conditions*, Detroit Free Press, December 9th, 2018, https://www.freep.com/story/sports/nfl/lions/2018/12/09/detroit-lions-state-farm-stadium-grass/2261468002/

CHAPTER 2.

1. Hynd, N., *Giant-sized confession: a groundskeepers deeds*, in *Sports Illustrated Vault*. August 28, 1988, Sports Illustrated.

2. Johnson, R.A., *The Knuckleball Club, the extraordinary men who mastered baseball's most difficult pitch*. 2016, Lanham MD Rowman and Littlefield.

3. Ostler, D. *A flood of memories of 'Stick in '62*. 2013; Available from: http://www.sfgate.com/giants/ostler/article/A-flood-of-memories-of-Stick-in-62-5083362.php - photo-5626266

CHAPTER 3

1. Goldman, S., Poor ice conditions continue to be a concern for NHL players, arenas, in Sports Illustrated, 2017, https://www.si.com/tech-media/2017/02/28/concerns-about-nhl-ice-conditions

2. Clinton, J., Why there's no simple solution to the NHL's battle with bad ice in Hockey News, 2017, https://thehockeynews.com/news/article/why-there-s-no-simple-solution-to-the-nhl-s-battle-with-bad-ice

3. *Understanding the Impact of Humidity in an Ice Rink.* June,2014; Available from [https://www.orfa.com/Resources/Documents/librarydocs/guides_bp/Understanding Humidity in Ice Rinks June2014.pdf].

4. *Coyotes announce cancellation of preseason game vs LA on September 18.* September 17th, 2017; Available from [https://www.nhl.com/coyotes/news/coyotes-announce-cancellation-of-preseason-game-vs-la-on-sept-18/c-291117884].

5. Bottomley, A. *5 bizarre hockey games affected by poor ice conditions.* September 18, 2017; Available from [https://www.sportsnet.ca/hockey/nhl/5-bizarre-hockey-games-affected-poor-ice-conditions/].

6. Messing, J. *NHL Ice Conditions Become A Hot Topic Again After In-Game Disturbances.* October 26th, 2017; Available from [https://www.flohockey.tv/articles/5060454-nhl-ice-conditions-become-a-hot-topic-again-after-in-game-disturbances].

7. Darnay, M. *Ten years ago today, Sidney Crosby won the Inaugural Winter Classic for the Penguins.* January 1, 2018; Available from [https://www.pensburgh.com/2018/1/1/16838716/penguins-2008-winter-classic-buffalo-snow-shootout-sidney-crosby].

8. Jansky, D. In Year 2, Barclays Center Ice Still a Problem, October 22, 2016, https://www.lighthousehockey.com/2016/10/22/13369316/barclays-center-ice-islanders-complaints

CHAPTER 4

1. *NHL History of Rinks.* Available from
   [http://www.frozenfaceoff.net/2015/01/nhl-history-of-rinks.html].

2. Weiner, E. *Not every 200 foot by 85 foot NHL rink is the same.* 2009 October 9th, 2009; Available from
   [https://www.nhl.com/news/not-every-200-foot-by-85-foot-nhl-rink-is-the-same/c-501626].

3. Swartz, T.B. and Arce, A., *New Insights Involving the Home Team Advantage.* International Journal of Sports Science and Coaching, 2014. 9: p. 681-692.

4. Stock, C., Home ice not so advantageous, March 2, 2009, Edmonton Journal.

5. Fischer, E. *What is "Having the Last Change" in Hockey?* June 3, 2016; Available from
   [http://dearsportsfan.com/2013/06/03/what-is-having-the-last-change-in-hockey/].

6. Goss, N. *How Much Does Home Ice Matter in the Stanley Cup Playoffs?* May 6th, 2013; Available from
   [https://bleacherreport.com/articles/1630882-how-much-does-home-ice-matter-in-the-stanley-cup-playoffs].

7. Sisk, C., *Nashville goes nuts for hockey and the predators* in *National Public Radio Morning Edition*, C. SIsk, Editor. 2017, National Public Radio

8. Staff, P.T. *How loud is it? Game 5 decibel readings.* June 7th, 2010; Available from
   [https://www.nhl.com/blackhawks/news/how-loud-is-it-game-5-decibel-readings/c-531107].

9. Vollman, R., *Stat-Shot.* 2016: ECW Press

10. Barrett, D. *NHL Column: Home ice advantage important so far in playoffs* April 18th, 2018; Available from
    [http://dailycampus.com/stories/2018/4/18/nhl-column-418-home-ice-advantage-important-so-far-in-playoffs].

CHAPTER 5

1. Pantic N. Americans Continue to Fight a Losing Battle on Clay. Tennis Magazine2017, http://www.tennis.com/pro-game/2017/04/clay-courts-roland-garros-atp-tennis-wta-tennis-serena-williams/65362/ .

2. Cervantes M. What Tennis Pros Don't Teach: Wisdom Tennis 101: Xlibris; 2015, https://www.xlibris.com/bookstore/bookdetail.aspx?bookid=SKU-000758159

3. USGS. Catoctin Formation - Metabasalt. USGS; 2017, https://mrdata.usgs.gov/geology/state/sgmc-unit.php?unit=VACAZc%3B0 .

4. Hanssen P. Court Construction & Maintenance Guide: Red or Green? Tennis Industry 2016. http://www.tennisindustrymag.com/articles/2016/03/13_court_construction_maintena.html

5. Golden Ocala. The history of clay tennis courts. September 20th, 2016.https://www.goldenocala.com/blog/tennis/the-history-of-clay-tennis-courts/

6. Newcomb T. With Roland Garros construction in limbo, clay courts still need care. Sports Illustrated May 14th, 2015. https://www.si.com/tennis/2015/05/14/roland-garros-construction-french-open-clay-courts-surface

7. Goyette K. A look at Rafael Nadal's French Open dominance. In: News TS, editor.June 10th, 2018, http://www.sportingnews.com/us/tennis/news/rafael-nadal-french-open-roland-garros-paris-clay-grand-slam-title/1fwmn4ebo85wi1ayiqb3ytzgw1

8. Rossingh D. Rafael Nadal: Why the "King of Clay" reigns in Paris. In: CNN, editor. June 1, 2018. https://www.cnn.com/2018/06/01/sport/rafael-nadal-pat-cash-mats-wilander-fench-open-roland-garros/index.html

9. Lundy A. The Secret To Nadal's Dominance On Clay. In: FiveThirtyEight, editor. June 1, 2018, https://fivethirtyeight.com/features/the-secret-to-nadals-dominance-on-clay/

CHAPTER 6

1. Kelley, B. *Augusta National Membership: Applying, the Costs and the Members.* April 13th, 2017; Available from: https://www.thoughtco.com/augusta-national-membership-1563545.

2. Strege, J. *How does Augusta National look in the summer? It isn't (as) pretty.* Available from: https://www.golfdigest.com/story/how-does-augusta-national-look-in-the-summer-it-isnt-as-pretty.

3. Lahnert, L., *Augusta National Closed in the Summer*, in *Amarillo Globe-News.* April 8th, 2010, accessed in 2017.

4. Kerr-Dineen, L. *7 ways to play Augusta National without being a member* 8/13/2018]; Available from: https://www.golfdigest.com/gallery/how-to-play-augusta-photos - 1.

5. Pye, S. *Larry Mize's life at the Masters: course worker, champion and 35-year veteran.* April 5th, 2018; Available from: https://www.theguardian.com/sport/that-1980s-sports-blog/2018/apr/05/masters-larry-mize-augusta-golf-champion.

6. Horrow, R. Augusta National masters art of minimal sponsorship, Reuters, April 6th, 2016, https://www.reuters.com/article/us-golf-masters-sponsors/augusta-national-masters-art-of-minimal-sponsorship-idUSKCN0X31SU

7. 1934 Masters, Wikipedia,2018, https://en.wikipedia.org/wiki/1934_Masters_Tournament

8. 1940 Masters, Wikipedia, 2018,
   https://en.wikipedia.org/wiki/1940_Masters_Tournament
9. 1960 Masters, Wikipedia, 2018,
   https://en.wikipedia.org/wiki/1960_Masters_Tournament
10. 2000 Masters, Wikipedia, 2018,
    https://en.wikipedia.org/wiki/2000_Masters_Tournament
11. 2010 Masters, Wikipedia, 2018,
    https://en.wikipedia.org/wiki/2010_Masters_Tournament

CHAPTER 7

1. Wikipedia. *Panathenaic Stadium.* 2018; Available from:
   https://en.wikipedia.org/wiki/Panathenaic_Stadium -
   1896_Olympics.
2. Cohen, S. *The 15 most awesome running tracks from
   around the world.* Janji June 4, 2015; Available from:
   http://info.runjanji.com/blog/15-most-unique-running-
   tracks-in-the-world.
3. Wikipedia. *Franklin Field.* 2018; Available from:
   https://en.wikipedia.org/wiki/Franklin_Field.
4. @pennrelays. *Today's attendance: 47,756 -- for a three-day
   total of 108,755. Thank you to the best track and field fans
   in the world! #TrackNation TWEET.* April 28th, 2018.
5. Wikipedia. *List of track and field stadiums by capacity.*
   2018; Available from: https://en.wikipedia.org/wiki/
   List_of_track_and_field_stadiums_by_capacity.
6. Oregon. *Hayward Field Renovation.* 2018; Available from:
   https://hayward.uoregon.edu/about.
7. Bullis, R.O. *Oregon vs Washington State, 1966.* 1966;
   Available from: https://www.youtube.com/watch?
   v=AnFaZ4KsoGs&feature=youtu.be.
8. Hermann, A. *These 10 things all happened at Oregon's
   historic Hayward Field.* June 4th, 2018; Available from:
   https://www.ncaa.com/news/trackfield-outdoor-

men/article/2018-06-03/these-10-things-all-happened-oregons-historic-hayward.

9. Wikipedia. *Steve Prefontaine.* 2018; Available from: https://en.wikipedia.org/wiki/Steve_Prefontaine.

10. Meyer, J., *Traditions are time-tested at historic Hayward...*, in *Denver Post.* June 28th, 2008: Denver CO.

11. Shannon, R. *Hayward Field Flashback: Mary Decker's Improbable 10k World Record.* March 18th, 2012; Available from: https://bleacherreport.com/articles/1107487-hayward-field-flashback-mary-deckers-improbable-10k-world-record.

12. USATF. *2016 US Olympic Team `trials-Track and Field.* 2016; Available from: http://www.usatf.org/Events---Calendar/2016/U-S--Olympic-Team-Trials---Track---Field/Results.aspx.

13. Wikipedia. *Athletics at the 2016 Summer Olympics Men's 200 metres.* 2018; Available from: https://en.wikipedia.org/wiki/Athletics_at_the_2016_Summer_Olympics_%E2%80%93_Men%27s_200_metres.

14. Andrews, R., Altitude had major impact on performances at Mexico City Olympic Games, Global Sports Matters website, October 11th, 2018, https://globalsportmatters.com/mexico/2018/10/11/altitude-major-impact-performances-mexico-city-olympic-games/

15. Bassett, D. R., Scientific contributions of A. V. Hill: exercise physiology pioneer, 1 November 2002, Journal of Applied Physiology, 2002, 92:1567-1572.

CHAPTER 8

1. *Laws of cricket* 2018; Available from [https://en.wikipedia.org/wiki/Laws_of_Cricket].

2. ESPN. *Longest Individual innings (by minutes)*. September 21, 2018; Available from [http://stats.espncricinfo.com/wi/content/records/284006 .html].

3. Usman, H., M.M. Hamza, P.M. Mamid, and T. Ahmad, *Improvement of geotechnical properties of cricket pitches*. Journal of Civil and Environmental Engineering 2016. 6. p. 256.

4. BR. *Pitch Perfect*. Game Theory, the Economist 2012 December 4th, 2012; Available from [https://www.economist.com/game-theory/2012/12/04/pitch-perfect].

5. K., A.A., How do you tamper with a cricket ball in The Economist October 31st, 2013, https://www.economist.com/the-economist-explains/2013/10/31/how-do-you-tamper-with-a-cricket-ball

6. MJ. *Cheating in Cricket, A ball tampering row consumes Australia*. The Economist 2018 March 28th 2018; Available from [https://www.economist.com/game-theory/2018/03/28/a-ball-tampering-row-consumes-australia].

7. Newlands, A., Steve Smith admits to Australia ball-tampering plan against South Africa March 24th 2018, The Guardian, https://www.theguardian.com/sport/2018/mar/24/cameron-bancroft-ball-tampering-claims-mar-south-africa-v-australia

8. Lavalette, T., Cricket's Confusion Over Cheating, in Forbes, July 14th, 2018, https://www.forbes.com/sites/tristanlavalette/2018/07/14/crickets-confusion-over-cheating/ - 3afeff656b36

9. Fuss, F.K., *Cricket balls: construction, non-linear visco-elastic properties, quality control and implications for the game*. Sport Technology 2008. **1**: p. 41-55.

CHAPTER 9

1. Bowen, M. *Seven ways NFL players keep from freezing.* 2016; Available from: http://www.espn.com/nfl/story/_/id/14525394/seven-ways-nfl-players-stay-warm-frigid-conditions-nfl.

2. Hartman, S., *Hartman: Bud Grant downplays cold's impact on teams*, in *Star Tribune*. 2016.

3. Pro reference football.com, data mined from individual years on the data site https://www.pro-football-reference.com

4. Garber, J. Brooklyn's Barclays Center might have the worst seat in American professional sports, October 12th, 2015, https://www.businessinsider.com/barclays-center-new-york-islanders-seats-2015-10

5. Boniello, K, and D. Balsimini, Fans sue Barclays Center over 'exceedingly dangerous' cheap seats, September 16th, 2017, https://nypost.com/2017/09/16/barclays-center-sued-by-injured-fans-over-exceedingly-steep-upper-level/

6. Kreda, A., Until New Arena Is Done, Islanders Will Play Part-Time at Nassau Coliseum, New York Times, January 29th, 2018, https://www.nytimes.com/2018/01/29/sports/hockey/islanders-nassau-coliseum-barclays-center.html

7. Beard, R. Pistons see bump in ticket sales despite empty seats, The Detroit News, February 16th, 2018, https://www.detroitnews.com/story/sports/nba/pistons/2018/02/16/pistons-bump-ticket-sales-fails-eye-test/110500410/

8. Donohue, D. M., Dome Team Performance in the NFL, New York City Data Science Academy, November 4th, 2015, https://www.datasciencecentral.com/profiles/blogs/dome-team-performance-in-the-nfl

CHAPTER 10

1. Bohn, M.K., *When Arnold Palmer saved the British Open from itself*, in *West Virginia Gazette/Associated Press* June 15th 2011.https://www.wvgazettemail.com/when-arnold-palmer-saved-the-british-open-from-itself/article_0fae9d5a-019f-5b17-b55b-1b55738fb1bf.html

2. The Open Championship, 2018, Wikipedia, https://en.wikipedia.org/wiki/The_Open_Championship

3. Old English translator, 2018, http://www.majstro.com/dictionaries/Old%20English-English/hlinc

4. The Royal and Ancient Golf Club, 2018, https://www.randa.org/Heritage/The-Royal-Ancient/The-Royal-Ancient-Golf-Club

5. The British Golf Museum at Saint Andrews , 2018, https://www.britishgolfmuseum.co.uk/

6. Kasinitz, A, How U.S. Open prize money has changed over the years, June 16th 2016, Pennsylvania Sports, https://www.pennlive.com/sports/index.ssf/2016/06/how_us_open_prize_money_has_ch.html

7. 1960 Master's Tournament, Wikipedia, 2018, https://en.wikipedia.org/wiki/1960_Masters_Tournament

8. Corrigan, J., The Open: 10 greatest finishes, The Telegraph (UK), July 14th, 2016, https://www.telegraph.co.uk/golf/2016/07/14/the-open-10-greatest-finishes/

9. Harig, B., Tiger Woods won't forget 81 in 2002, ESPN.com, July 15th, 2013, http://www.espn.com/golf/theopen/story/_/id/9466803/tiger-woods-recalls-dreadful-third-round-open-muirfield-2002-golf

10. golf.com, Hardy souls who endured worst day of major

weather ever recall third round at 2002 Open, GOlf.com, July 15th, 2013, https://www.golf.com/tour-and-news/third-round-2002-british-open-was-worst-major-weather-ever

11. Donegan, L., Old fogey' Tom Watson falls at last hole of 2009 Open, The Guardian, July 19th, 2009, https://www.theguardian.com/sport/2009/jul/19/clink-tom-watson-open-golf

CHAPTER 11

1. Dilworth, M., *America's Cup 2017: how does it work, who is the favourite, and how can I watch it?*, in *The Telegraph.* 2016: London.

2. *The America's Cup.* 2017; Available from [https://en.wikipedia.org/wiki/America%27s_Cup].

3. Harvey, M., *How technology helps racing yachts sail faster than wind*, in *The Telegraph* (UK). May 30th, 2017: London, UK.

4. Johnson, J.S. *Columbia and Shamrock.* 1899; Available from [https://www.loc.gov/item/2016813178/].

CHAPTER 12

1. MLB. *Official Baseball Rules.* 2018; [http://mlb.mlb.com/documents/0/8/0/268272080/2018_Official_Baseball_Rules.pdf].

2. Engineering Index. *Wood Density.* 2018; [https://www/engineeringtoolbox.com/wood-density-d-40.html].

3. Brown, T. *Baseball Hall of Fame: Vladimir Guerrero, bat whisperer.* July 25th, 2018;

[https://sports.yahoo.com/baseball-hall-fame-vladimir-guerrero-bat-whisperer-155906729.html].

4. Harris, W.H. *Does a corked bat really hit farther?* June 28, 2012; [<https://entertainment.howstuffworks.com/corked-bat-hit-ball-farther.htm>].

5. Solomon, C. *The physics of cheating in baseball.* June 23rd, 2011; [https://www.smithsonianmag.com/science-nature/the-physics-of-cheating-in-baseball-19613464/].

6. Petchesky, B. *This is Pete Rose's corked bat.* June 8th, 2010; Available from [https://deadspin.com/5555714/this-is-pete-roses-corked-bat].

7. Schaall, E. *MLB: 7 Hitters Who Will Go Down in History as Cheaters.* November 12th 2016; [https://www.cheatsheet.com/sports/7-mlb-batters-whose-cheating-exploits-live-in-infamy.html/].

8. Engber, D., How to throw the goopball, in Slate, October 23rd, 2006, http://www.slate.com/articles/news_and_politics/explainer/2006/10/how_to_throw_the_goopball.html

9. Schaall, E. *MLB: 7 Pitchers Who Will Go Down in History as Cheaters.* August 12th, 2015; [https://www.cheatsheet.com/sports/most-likely-2019-stanley-cup-matchups-according-to-vegas.html/].

10. Hayhurst, D. *A Major League Pitcher's Guide To Doctoring A Baseball.* April 11th, 2014; [https://deadspin.com/a-major-league-pitchers-guide-to-doctoring-a-baseball-1562307090].

11. Sheinin, D., Why the drop in home runs in 2018? Major League Baseball had better hope it's the weather. April 20th, 2018, Salt Lake City Tribune, https://www.sltrib.com/sports/2018/04/20/why-the-drop-in-home-runs-in-2018-major-league-baseball-had-better-hope-its-the-weather/

12. Edwards, J., Could humidors be the solution to MLB's home

run 'problem', May 25th, 2018, The Sporting News,
http://www.sportingnews.com/us/mlb/news/mlb-baseball-
study-investigation-humidors-/827449ntnjfo11dida5jzpwgg

13. Stark, J., As La Russa talks, the smudge mark thickens,
October 23rd, , 2006, ESPN,
http://www.espn.com/mlb/playoffs2006/columns/story?
columnist=stark_jayson&id=2636469

CHAPTER 13

1. Abramson, M., *Knicks DeflateGate? Phil Jackson said 1973
NBA champion Knicks deflated basketballs*, in *New York
Daily News*. 2015,
https://www.nydailynews.com/sports/basketball/knicks/k
nicks-deflategate-phil-jackson-73-team-deflated-balls-
article-1.2095137

2. Smith, S., *Skill could be cheating teams get away with*, in
Bangor Daily News. December 12th, 1986: Bangor ME.,
https://news.google.com/newspapers?
nid=2457&dat=19861212&id=AKhJAAAAIBAJ&sjid=J
A4NAAAAIBAJ&pg=6821,986502

3. Berman, M., *Bill Bradley cops to deflating balls in Knicks
glory days*, in *New York Post*. January 30th, 2015,
https://nypost.com/2015/01/30/bill-bradley-cops-to-
deflating-balls-in-knicks-glory-days/

4. Curtis, C., *Deflategate 2? N.J.'s Shaquille O'Neal admits to
taking air out of basketballs during career*, in *NJ Advance
Media*. June 8th, 2015,
https://www.nj.com/knicks/index.ssf/2015/06/deflategat
e_2_njs_shaquille_oneal_admits_to_taking.html

5. Viera, M., *Home Court Advantage begins with the ball*, in
The New York Times. March 2, 2012, New York Times
Publishing.https://www.nytimes.com/2012/03/02/sports/
ncaabasketball/college-home-teams-can-pick-their-brands-

of-basketballs.html?
mtrref=www.google.com&gwh=1BB29543EFF0F162701
C72590428B3D9&gwt=pay

6. Brinson, W., Report: Patriots coaches admit team stole play
sheets during Spygate era, CBS Sports, September 8th,
2015, https://www.cbssports.com/nfl/news/report-
patriots-coaches-admit-team-stole-play-sheets-during-
spygate-era/

7. Sonny, J., Report: Patriots coaches admit team stole play
sheets during Spygate era, January 19th, 2015, EliteDaily,
https://www.elitedaily.com/sports/history-new-england-
patriots-allegedly-cheating/910436

CHAPTER 14

1. Reeves, E. *Slow death of a fast game.* July 25th, 2009;
Available from
[https://www.theguardian.com/sport/2009/jul/26/cesta-
punta-basque-sport].

2. *Jai Alai.* 2018; Available from [http://www.fla-
gaming.com/jai-alai-2/].

3. Gonzalez-Abrisketa, O., *A Basque-American Deep Game:
The Political Economy of Ethnicity and Jai-Alai in the
United States.* Studia Iberica et Americana (SIBA), 2017.
4: p. 179-198.

4. Kurlansky, M., *The Basque History of the World* 1999,
New York, NY: Penguin Books,

5. Israel, D.K. *5 Odd Balls.* October 11th, 2011; Available
from [http://mentalfloss.com/article/28960/5-odd-balls].8

6. Copertone, C. and P. Eguiluz, *Beti Jai: The Last Surviving
Basque Pelota Historic Fronton in Madrid.* MAS Context,
2015. 28: p. 102-121.

7. FrontonBetiJaiMadrid. *Salvemos el Fronton Beti-Jai.* 2017;
Available from [http://frontonbetijaimadrid.org].

8. *Jai alai frontons in the USA.* 2017; Available from [http://www.fla-gaming.com/jai-alai-frontons-in-the-usa/].

9. Gonzalez-Abrisketa, O., *Jai Alai in the United States,* in Recovered Memories, Spain, New Orleans, and support for the American Revolution, Guerrera-Acosta, J. M., ed, 2017, pp 325-334.

CHAPTER 15

1. Schenau, v.I., *A power balance applied to speedskating,* in *Kinesiology.* 1981, Free University of Amsterdam.My Book

2. De Koning, J.J. *Slapeskate history and background.* 1997; Available from: http://www.sportsci.org/news/news9703/slapxtra.htm.

3. *World record progression 5000M speed skating women.* 2017; Available from: https://en.wikipedia.org/wiki/World_record_progression_5000_m_speed_skating_women.

4. Loudin, A., Why Olympic skaters move from wheels to ice, Outside Magazine, February 9th 2018, https://www.outsideonline.com/2280241/why-olympic-skaters-move-wheels-ice

5. Block, M., Maame Biney Came To The U.S. From Ghana At 5. Now 18, She's A Team USA Speedskater, National Public Radio, February 12th, 2018, https://www.npr.org/sections/thetorch/2018/02/12/585039149/maame-biney-came-to-the-u-s-from-ghana-at-5-now-18-shes-a-team-usa-speedskater

6. Apolo Ohno, Wikipedia, 2018, https://en.wikipedia.org/wiki/Apolo_Ohno

7. Short Track Speedskating, Wikipedia 2018, https://en.wikipedia.org/wiki/Short_track_speed_skating

8. Pilon, M., To Go Further, Speedskaters Had to Let Go of

Their Wheels, NY Times, February 10th, 2014, https://www.nytimes.com/2014/02/11/sports/olympics/to-go-further-speedskaters-had-to-let-go-of-their-wheels.html

9. Mayer, J., The History of Ice Skates, Science Friday, March 4th, 2018, https://www.sciencefriday.com/articles/history-ice-skates/

10. International Skating Union, 2018, https://www.isu.org/

CHAPTER 16

1. KaysCurling. *Ailsa Craig- The world's best granite.* 2018; Available from [https://www.kayscurling.com/ailsa-craig-granite.html].

2. Tait, C., How scouts study curling stones to help give pros an edge, April 27th, 2018, The Toronto Globe and Mail https://www.theglobeandmail.com/canada/alberta/article-how-scouts-study-curling-stones-to-help-give-pros-an-edge/

3. Owens, B. *New broom technology sweeps through curling world* 2015; Available from [https://www.insidescience.org/news/new-broom-technology-sweeps-through-curling-world].

4. Pauls, K. and C. MacIntosh. *Top curling teams say they won't use high-tech brooms.* 2015; Available from [http://www.cbc.ca/news/canada/manitoba/top-curling-teams-say-they-won-t-use-high-tech-brooms-1.3274903].

5. IceHalo. *The Ice Halo* 2018; Available from [http://www.icehalo.com/].

6. curling.com. *Curling's funnyman takes centre stage.* July 9th, 2015; Available from [https://www.curling.ca/blog/2015/07/09/curlings-funny-man-takes-centre-stage/].

7. Ouellette, J. *Here's the Physics Behind the 'Broomgate' Controversy Rocking the Sport of Curling.* June 12th, 2016;

Available from [https://gizmodo.com/heres-the-physics-behind-the-broomgate-controversy-rock-1781822352].

CHAPTER 17

1. Wikipedia. Ski. 2018; Available from: https://en.wikipedia.org/wiki/Ski

2. Fessl, S. A brief history of skis. JSTOR February 14th, 2018; Available from: https://daily.jstor.org/brief-history-skis/

3. Masia, S. Grip and Glide, A Short HIstory of Ski Wax. accessed 2018; Available from: https://www.skiinghistory.org/history/grip-and-glide-short-history-ski-wax.

4. Leger-Dionne, F. Behind the Scenes with Canadian Wax Chief Yves Bilodeau (in English). July 24th, 2014; Available from: http://fasterskier.com/fsarticle/behind-the-scenes-with-canadian-wax-chief-yves-bilodeau-in-english/

5. Gaines, C. It's so cold at the Winter Olympics that skiers are being forced to throw away their expensive skis after practice runs. February 8th, 2018; Available from: https://www.businessinsider.com/winter-olympics-Weather-its-cold-2018-2.

6. Slalom, Learn more about slalom, Merriam Webster Dictionary Online, 2018, https://www.merriam-webster.com/dictionary/slalom

7. Gondola, Dictionary.com, 2018, https://www.dictionary.com/browse/gondola

8. Finiculaire, Collins Dictionary, 2018, https://www.collinsdictionary.com/us/dictionary/french-english/funiculaire

9. Nordic Ski Lingo, Eb's adventure, November 13, 2015, https://ebsadventure.com/blogs/news/56854721-nordic-ski-lingo

CHAPTER 18

1. Barrow, J.D. *Why ban full-body olympics swimsuits? A scientist explains polyurethane.* The Daily Beast 2012 7-25-2012; Available from [https://www.thedailybeast.com/why-ban-full-body-olympics-swimsuits-a-scientist-explains-polyurethane].

2. Pendergrast, D.R., J.C. Mollendorf, R. Cuviello, and A.C. Termin, *Application of theoretical principles to swimsuit drag reduction.* Sports Engineering, 2006. 9: p. 65-76.

3. Morrison, J. *Spanx on Steroids: How Speedo Created the New Record-Breaking Swimsuit.* June 26th, 20112; Available from [https://www.smithsonianmag.com/science-nature/spanx-on-steroids-how-speedo-created-the-new-record-breaking-swimsuit-9662/].

4. Tang, S.K.Y. *The Rocket Swimsuit: Speedo's LZR Racer.* Science in the News 2008; Available from [http://sitn.hms.harvard.edu/flash/2008/issue47-2/].

5. Foster, L., D. James, and S. Haake, *Influence of full body swimsuits on competitive performance.* Procedia Engineering, 2012. 34: p. 712-717.

6. NCAA. *NCAA Committees endorse swimsuit restrictions.* 29 July, 2009; Available from [https://www.swimmingworldmagazine.com/news/ncaa-committees-endorse-swimsuit-restrictions/].

7. NCAA. *Swimming and Diving 2017-2018 and 2018-2019 rules and interpretations* 2017; Available from [http://www.csoaofficials.com/csoaquiz/rulebook.pdf].

8. AP. *Diana Nyad defends Cuba-to-Florida swim as skeptics question use of gear.* September 11th, 2013; Available from [https://www.theguardian.com/sport/2013/sep/11/diana-nyad-defends-swim-from-skeptics].

9. LongSwimsDatabase. *Diana Nyad*. 2018; Available from [https://db.marathonswimmers.org/p/diana-nyad/].

CHAPTER 19

1. Fontanella, J., *The Physics of Basketball*. 2006: Johns Hopkins University Press.
2. Barzikina, I. *The Physics of an Optimal Basketball Free throw*. arXiv.org February 21st, 2017; Available from: https://arxiv.org/abs/1702.07234.
3. Strelow, B., *Basket Case: Do soft rims exist? Answers found in basketball-style 'MythBusters*, in *Winston Salem Journal*. March 3rd, 2017.
4. O'Connell, R. *Proof that the Maui Invitational's soft rims make it paradise for shooters*. November 21st, 2017; Available from: basketball/2017/11/21/16685072/maui-invitational-rims-soft-juiced-notre-dame-wichita-state.
5. NCAA. *NCAA Basketball 2013-2014 and 2014-2015 rules*. August, 2013; Available from: https://ncaambb.arbitersports.com/Groups/104883/Library/files/BR15.pdf.
6. Stein, M. *Rim shot: NBA scoring on the rise*. November 4th, 2009; Available from: http://www.espn.com/nba/news/story?id=4620192.
7. Krause, J.R. *Annual Research Report Of the NABC Research Committee*. March, 2002; Available from: http://grfx.cstv.com/photos/schools/nabc/genrel/auto_pdf/NABCResearch2002AnnualReport.pdf.
8. Steinbach, P. *Manufacturers Continue to Improve the Basketball Goal*. March, 2006; Available from: https://www.athleticbusiness.com/Gym-Fieldhouse/goal-oriented.html.
9. DraperInc, Gymnasium Equipment Court Design and Rules, NCAA, 2016,

https://webcache.googleusercontent.com/search?
q=cache:RNf1xJ-Q-
xkJ:https://www.draperinc.com/documentdownload.aspx
%3Fpath%3Dimages/Catalogs/WhitePapers%26file%3D
Gym_Court_Design_Rules-
NCAA_0916.pdf+&cd=8&hl=en&ct=clnk&gl=us&client=
firefox-b-1-ab

10. About Spalding(R) Equipment, 2018,
    https://www.spaldingequipment.com/about.aspx

CHAPTER 20

1. Ritter, J., Paul Azinger Reveals why the U.S. Wins the
   Presidents Cup but not the Ryder Cup, Golf.com, October
   7th, 2015, https://www.golf.com/golf-plus/paul-azinger-
   reveals-why-us-wins-presidents-cup-not-ryder-cup

2. Harig, B, No U.S. road wins in Ryder Cup for 25 years --
   why has it been so long?, ESPN, September 17th, 2018,
   http://www.espn.com/golf/story/_/id/24803175/ryder-
   cup-2018-why-team-usa-not-won-road-25-years.

3. Souhan, J, Shame on American fans who have turned part
   of Ryder Cup gallery into a mob, Minneapolis Star
   Tribune, October 2nd, 2016,
   http://www.startribune.com/shame-on-american-fans-
   who-have-turned-part-of-the-golf-gallery-into-a-
   mob/395536261/

4. Viner, B, From polite applause to wild catcalls: how Ryder
   Cup fans have changed, The Independent, September
   25th, 2012,
   https://www.independent.co.uk/sport/golf/from-polite-
   applause-to-wild-catcalls-how-ryder-cup-fans-have-
   changed-8168212.html

5. Kerr-Dineen, L., Don't blame the entire Ryder Cup crowd
   because of a few idiots, USA Today, October 2nd 2016,

https://ftw.usatoday.com/2016/10/2016-us-ryder-cup-
crowd-hazeltine-video-american-fans-european-reaction-
rory-mcilroy

6. Kerr-Dineen, L., Pro golfer's wife speaks out against
disrespectful U.S. crowd after Presidents Cup win, USA
TOday, October 5th, 2017 ,
https://ftw.usatoday.com/2017/10/pro-golfers-wife-marc-
leishman-presidents-cup-us-fans

7. Williams, R., US fan called out, and holes out!,
RyderCup.com, September 29th, 2016,
https://www.rydercup.com/news-media/europe/us-fan-
called-out-and-holes-out-o

CHAPTER 21

1. McCaffrey, M., M. Keenan, A. Fagot, ., G. Peterson, A.
Rey, J. Simcoe, and C. Vollmer. *PwC Sports Outlook.* 2017;
Available from
[https://www.pwc.com/us/en/industry/entertainment-
media/publications/assets/pwc-sports-outlook-2017.pdf].

2. Brautigan, B. and N. DeSantis, *Here's How Every NBA
Team Makes Its Money, Visualized.* Forbes, March
21st, 2016.

3. *Astrodome.* 2018; Available from
[https://en.wikipedia.org/wiki/Astrodome].

4. Devine, D. *Pelicans coach Monty Williams thinks Oracle
Arena's so loud it might be illegal.* Ball don't lie April 20th,
2015; Available from [https://sports.yahoo.com/pelicans-
coach-monty-williams-thinks-oracle-arena-s-so-loud-it-
might-be-illegal-195047667.html?y20=1].

5. Pollakoff, B. *Marv Albert says it seems like Celtics are
pumping in artificial crowd noise.* NBC Sports January
26th 2013; Available from
[https://nba.nbcsports.com/2013/01/26/marv-albert-says-

it-seems-like-celtics-are-pumping-in-artificial-crowd-noise/].

6. Dwyer, K. *Wizards broadcaster Steve Buckhantz rips the Miami Heat for adding 'canned crowd noise'*. Ball don't lie October 30th, 2014; Available from [https://sports.yahoo.com/wizards-broadcaster-steve-buckhantz-rips-the-miami-heat-for-adding--canned-crowd-noise---video-160801233.html?y20=1].

7. Ahlgren, A., Why the NFL Stadium Experience Is Dying, in Bleacher Report, May 22nd, 2012, https://bleacherreport.com/articles/1191009-why-the-nfl-stadium-experience-is-dying

8. Orioles promotion offers free tickets to kids for entire season, April 6th, 2018, Baltimore Sun, http://www.baltimoresun.com/sports/orioles/bs-sp-orioles-kids-promotion-0406-story.html

9. *Orioles Field Promotions* 2018; Available from [https://www.mlb.com/orioles/tickets/specials].

10. Jones, L. H., Falcons fined, lose draft pick for using fake crowd noise, USA Today, March, 15th, 2015, https://www.usatoday.com/story/sports/nfl/falcons/2015/03/30/rich-mckay-suspension-draft-pick-piping-crowd-noise/70667254/

11. Scacco, M., 7 NBA players known for trash talking with Spike Lee at the Garden, New York Daily News, November 9th, 2015, https://www.nydailynews.com/sports/basketball/7-nba-players-trashing-talking-spike-lee-article-1.2428467

12. Arnovitz, K, The NBA's next big cash grab: Taking over your downtown, ESPN.com, November 13th, 2018. http://www.espn.com/nba/story/_/id/25218998/the-nba-real-estate-company-now

13. Felt, H., $100 to not see games? The Warriors' 'In the Building' pass is Silicon Valley in ticket form, The Guardian, November 13th, 2018,

https://www.theguardian.com/sport/2018/nov/13/golden
-state-warriors-nba-in-the-building-pass

14. Grathoff, P., Royals will give fans a shot to win their season
tickets by hitting a homer at the K, The Kansas City Star,
September 28th, 2018,
https://www.kansascity.com/sports/mlb/kansas-city-
royals/article219002970.html

CHAPTER 22

1. Borzi, P. *Line of Sight*. May 14th, 2014; Available from:
http://www.sportsonearth.com/article/75655494/baseball
-batters-eye-can-impact-hitting-success-and-safety.

2. Wikipedia. *Tony Conigliaro*. 2018; Available from:
https://en.wikipedia.org/wiki/Tony_Conigliaro.

3. MLB. *Red sox single ticket pricing*. 2018; Available from:
https://www.mlb.com/redsox/tickets/single-game-
tickets/pricing.

4. Jere. *TV Eye*. 2007; Available from:
http://letsgosox.blogspot.com/2007/08/tv-eye.html.

5. Bollinger, R., Trees return to Target Field, MLB.com, April
14th, 2014, https://www.mlb.com/news/trees-return-to-
target-field/c-70925924

6. Rosciak, T., Sun's glare may be reduced at Miller Park,
Milwaukee Journal Sentinel, September 13th, 2013,
http://archive.jsonline.com/sports/brewers/suns-glare-
may-be-reduced-at-miller-park-b99974232Z1-
223712681.html/

7. Landers, C., Seven bizarre ballpark features from baseball
history that you'll need to see to believe, MLB.com,
September 20th, 2015, https://www.mlb.com/cut4/seven-
of-baseballs-weirdest-ballpark-features/c-144747404

8. Wikipedia, Wahconah Park, 2018,

https://www.mlb.com/cut4/seven-of-baseballs-weirdest-
ballpark-features/c-144747404

CHAPTER 23

1. Moskowitz, T.J. and L.J. Wertheim, *Scorecasting*. 2011,
   New York: Crown Publishing.
2. Dohmen, T.J., *In Support of the Supporters? Do Social
   Forces Shape Decisions of the Impartial?*, Institute for the
   Study of Labor. (Germany), Editor. 2003, IZA: Bonn.
3. Weisman, L., The NFL Modifies Instant Replay Again
   (And Again And Again), Twistitiy.com, March 29th, 2017,
   http://twistity.com/twistity-the-nfl-modifies-instant-replay-
   again-and-again-and-again/
4. Rumsby, B. Video replays used for first time during
   France's 3-1 friendly win over Italy as 'football history'
   made, The Telegraph, September 2nd 2016,
   https://www.telegraph.co.uk/football/2016/09/02/video-
   replays-used-for-first-time-during-frances-3-1-friendly-wi/
5. Goldberg, J. MLS leads the way among soccer leagues
   worldwide as it prepares to roll out video replay, The
   Oregonian, March 14th, 2017,
   https://www.oregonlive.com/timbers/index.ssf/2017/03/
   mls_leads_the_way_in_rolling_0.html
6. Johnson, D., How VAR made history with penalty for
   France, ESPN, June 16th, 2018,
   http://www.espn.com/soccer/world-cup-
   soccer/story/3528392/how-var-made-history-with-
   penalty-awarded-to-france-against-australia
7. Dubner, J., Football Freakonomics": How Advantageous Is
   Home-Field Advantage? And Why?, Freakonomics,
   December 18th, 2011,
   http://freakonomics.com/2011/12/18/football-

freakonomics-how-advantageous-is-home-field-
advantage-and-why/

8. NBA, NBA Referee Instant Replay Trigger Outline, 2018,
National Basketball Association,
http://www.nba.com/official/instant-replay-
guidelines.html#

9. Associated Press, Replay use expanded in hoops, ESPN,
June 23, 2013, http://www.espn.com/mens-college-
basketball/story/_/id/9419050/expansion-replay-review-
rule-changes-ncaa-hoops.

10. Wikipedia, Instant Replay, 2018,
https://en.wikipedia.org/wiki/Instant_replay

11. Rugby League International Federation, (RLIF),

12. The International Laws of the Game and Notes on the
Laws, 2018, http://www.therfl.co.uk/~therflc/clientdocs/
rugby_laws_book_2004_.pdf

CHAPTER 24

1. Stray-Gundersen J and B.D. Levine, *Living high-training
high and low" is equivalent to "living high-training low" for
sea-level performance.* Medicine and Science in Sports and
Exercise, 1997. 29: p. S136.

2. Howey, E., Tour de France 2018: How big of a problem is
doping in cycling?, Fansided, July 7th, 2018,
https://fansided.com/2018/07/07/tour-de-france-2018-
big-problem-doping-cycling/

3. *What is a normal hematocrit?* 2014; Available from:
http://www.emedicinehealth.com/hematocrit_blood_test/
page3_em.htm - what_is_a_normal_hematocrit.

4. Boning, D., N. Maassen, and A. Pries, *The Hematocrit
Paradox – How Does Blood Doping Really Work?* The
International Journal of Sports Medicine, 2011. 32: p.
242-246.

5. Sheppard, J.A. *Elevation Training Mask and the Effects: A Case Report*. 2012; Available from: http://www.trainingmask.com/news/25/Elevation-Training-Mask-and-the-Effects%3A-A-Case-Report.html.

6. Lundby, C., P. Robach, and B. Saltin, *The evolving science of detection of 'blood doping'*. British Journal of Pharmacology, 2012. 165: p. 1306-1315.

7. Union Cycliste Internationale, Inside the UCI, 2018, http://www.uci.org/inside-uci/clean-sport/anti-doping/uci-anti-doping-programme

8. World Anti-Doping Agency, (WADA), "The Prohibited List", 2018, https://www.wada-ama.org/en/what-we-do/the-prohibited-list

9. Sports Hyperbarics, Oxygen Deprivation Tents vs Hyperbaric Oxygen Chambers, 2018, https://sportshyperbarics.com/oxygen-deprivation-altitude-tents-vs-hyperbaric-chambers-therapy-hbot/ .

10. Meridian Valley Laboratories,2018, The relationship between blood pressure and blood viscosity, https://www.meridianvalleylab.com/the-relationship-between-blood-pressure-and-blood-viscosity/

11. American Medical Association, AMA Encourages More Patients to Know Numbers on World Hypertension Day, May 17th, 2018, https://www.ama-assn.org/ama-encourages-more-patients-know-numbers-world-hypertension-day

12. Baron, D. A., D. M. Martin, and S. A. Magd, Doping in sports and its spread to at-risk populations: an international review, 2007, World Psychiatry, 6(2), 118-123. https://www.ncbi.nlm.nih.gov/pmc/articles/PMC2219897/

13. Savulescu, J., B. Foddy, and M Clayton, Why we should allow performance enhancing drugs in sport, British Journal of Sports Medicine, 2004:36;666-670, https://bjsm.bmj.com/content/38/6/666?

utm_source=trendmd&utm_medium=cpc&utm_campaign
=bjsm&utm_content=consumer&utm_term=0-A

CHAPTER 25

1. Brulliard, K., This tennis tournament is using shelter dogs as ballboys, February 23rd, 2017, The Washington Post, https://www.washingtonpost.com/news/animalia/wp/2017/02/23/ this-tennis-tournament-is-using-shelter-dogs-as-ballboys/

2. Hyde, S. *Top 25 live animal mascots in college football.* Fox Sports October 20th, 2016; Available from [https://www.foxsports.com/college-football/gallery/best-live-animal-mascots-college-football-ncaa-bevo-ralphie-smokey-mike-the-tiger-uga-102215].

3. NorthwesternAthletics, The Evolution of Willie, in Northwestern Magazine, Fall 2014, https://www.northwestern.edu/magazine/fall2014/campuslife/then-the-evolution-of-willie.html

4. Commito, M. *How Detroit's Octopus-Tossing Tradition Started.* April 28th 2017; Available from [https://sports.vice.com/en_ca/article/nzawzq/how-detroits-octopus-tossing-tradition-started].

5. Wikipedia. *Legend of the Octopus.* 2018; Available from [https://en.wikipedia.org/wiki/Legend_of_the_Octopus].

6. Wikipedia. *Amphipoda.* 2018; Available from [https://en.wikipedia.org/wiki/Amphipoda].

7. Schmitt, B., Catfish tossing started because some Predators fans hated Detroit, April 13th, 2018, USA Today, https://www.tennessean.com/story/sports/nhl/predators/2018/04/12/nashville-predators- why-do-fans-throw-catfish-nhl-stanley-cup-playoffs-bridgestone-arena/508025002/

8. Ingram, M. *7 memorable things hockey fans have thrown on*

the ice. CBC Sports March 26th, 2015; Available from [https://www.cbc.ca/sports/hockey/nhl/7-memorable-things-hockey-fans-have-thrown-on-the-ice-1.3009747].

9. Richards, G., Rats!, a Florida Panthers playoff etiquette guide April 13th, 2016, Miami Herald, https://www.miamiherald.com/sports/nhl/florida-panthers/article71604227.html

10. Petchesky, B. *15 Years Ago Today, Randy Johnson Exploded A Bird.* March 24th, 2016; Available from [https://deadspin.com/15-years-ago-today-randy-johnson-exploded-a-bird-1766865936].

11. Curtis, C., Remembering when Manu Ginobili knocked down a live bat in the middle of an NBA game, August 27th, 2018, USA Today, https://ftw.usatoday.com/2018/08/manu-ginobili-retires-bat-game-halloween-video

12. Rhodes, B. *Bird flies off with golf ball.* Rules of Golf December 16th, 2014; Available from [http://www.barryrhodes.com/2014/12/bird-flies-off-with-golf-ball.html].

13. Reuters, Yachting: America's Cup crew hits whale, February 15th, 2005, New Zealand Herald, http://www.nzherald.co.nz/sport/news/article.cfm?c_id=4&objectid=10011133

14. Castrovince, A. *Bug game forever part of Tribe/Yanks Lore.* October 4th, 2017; Available from [https://www.mlb.com/news/bug-game-forever-part-of-tribe-yankees-lore/c-257346172].

15. Landers, C., Seven bizarre ballpark features from baseball history that you'll need to see to believe, MLB, September 20th, 2015, https://www.mlb.com/cut4/seven-of-baseballs-weirdest-ballpark-features/c-144747404

16. Mearns, A., Atlanta's first famous baseball park was also home to a giant magnolia tree in center field, MLB.com,

May 23rd, 2018, https://www.mlb.com/cut4/history-of-ponce-de-leon-park-in-atlanta/c-277672886

17. Wikipedia, Clark Field, 2018,
https://en.wikipedia.org/wiki/Clark_Field_(1928)

CHAPTER 26

1. Marchi, M. *The Stats Go Marching In: Bringing Back the Birdie Tebbetts Shift*. April 13th, 2010; Available from [https://www.baseballprospectus.com/news/article/16439/the-stats-go-marching-in-bringing-back-the-birdie-tebbetts-shift/].

2. BaseballAlmanac. *Box Score of game played on Saturday, May 22nd, 1954*. 2018; Available from [http://www.baseball-almanac.com/box-scores/boxscore.php?boxid=195405220SLN].

3. Lindbergh, B. *The Past, Present, and Future of Baseball's Most Daring Defense*. March 8th 2018; Available from [https://www.theringer.com/mlb/2018/3/9/17099736/mlb-preview-past-present-future-of-outfield-shifting-phillies].

4. MLB. *Dodgers use wall of infielders*. August 29th, 2014; Available from [https://www.mlb.com/video/dodgers-use-wall-of-infielders/c-35789081].

5. Gault, M. *7 teams that flourished with crazy formations*. February 10th, 2015; Available from [https://www.sportskeeda.com/slideshow/football-7-teams-successful-crazy-formations].

6. Wang, J., I Fox, J. Skaza, N. Linck, S. Singh, and J. Wiens, The Advantage of Doubling: A Deep Reinforcement Learning Approach to Studying the Double Team in the NBA, MIT Sloan Sports Analytics Conference, 2018 https://arxiv.org/abs/1803.02940

ACKNOWLEDGMENTS

Brian and Mike want to thank the staff and ancillary support at Fifth Avenue Press, including our editor Rich Reyti, as well as Erin Helmrich, Amanda Szot, and Maxine Thompson who helped with book layout, illustrations, factchecking, and all of the details of book production and publication. Your help was invaluable. We also want to thank the Ann Arbor District Library for giving us tremendous support. The book would not have been developed nearly as quickly or smoothly without the help of the library staff and involvement.

Brian and Mike would also like to thank a number of folks who read and/or helped critique chapters for us, including Olatz Gonzalez Abrisketa, Stefan Szymanski, John Cullen and Zuzana Tomas among others. We appreciate their help through the process. Our goal for the project was to produce a book that was factually accurate (the where, what and who) and to offer some subjective insights in each chapter, without being an endless bore. There is a wide variation in the authors' experiences and knowledge from more common sports that are included to more rare ones. We sought assistance from experts in the areas we required support and their efforts allowed us to provide the most accurate content. By covering a variety of competitive athletics, we were able to present common links in gaining advantage and show it as a much more universal phenomenon.

We would like to thank friends who came back to us with ideas of other stories that for time or page constraints could not be included. We've heard about the pink locker room in Ames, Iowa and changing the temperature inside arenas. Who knows? Maybe we will tackle badminton, lacrosse, rugby, sumo, kin-ball and table tennis, if a sequel is demanded. Again, the web site corkedthebook.com is the place to weigh in and say "I'd love to see stories on this or that" or, "Please, not another book!"

Brian wants to thank his wife, Nancy, and his kids, Francisco and Benjamin, and his extended family with whom he's observed home field advantage. He also wants to thank the parents of the kids teams he has coached for putting up with him as he applied his insights of competitive advantage to very low level coach- and kid-pitch baseball, and kindergarten level soccer, among others.

Mike would like to thank his wife, Liz, who acted as a first-pass editor and sounding board for many of the chapters, and his new son, Michael, who was an inspiration.

Finally we want to thank you, the reader, for taking an interest.

ABOUT THE AUTHORS

Brian Love is an Engineering Professor at Michigan and an AnnArborite. He also is a lifetime Cubs fan although he is now seen more often at Comerica than at Wrigley. *Corked* is Brian's 2nd book. On the side, Brian coaches youth sports for his kids teams where being available is more valued than knowing anything about said sport.

Michael Burns is a researching clinician in the Department of Anesthesiology in the School of Medicine at the University of Michigan. He is an avid Detroit sports fan and follows major and minor league affiliates. As a new first-time father, Michael is excited for opportunities to share his love for sports with his son.

Made in the USA
Middletown, DE
13 April 2019